Understanding Your

Parents

UNDERSTANDING YOUR

PARENTS

HAROLD A. RASHKIS, M.D.

LEVON D. TASHJIAN, M.D.

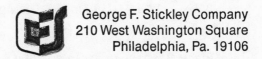 George F. Stickley Company
210 West Washington Square
Philadelphia, Pa. 19106

Contents

Contents (Continued)

Oh, what a tangled web do parents
weave
When they think that their children are
naive

Ogden Nash, *What Makes the Sky Blue?*

Foreword

The concept of this book is quite simple. It is our purpose to turn the tables and offer to adolescents a "primer on parents." We want to take a good look at parents, especially to look at those irrational and often unconscious forces within them which cause them to behave in the ways they do toward their young. Furthermore, we want to examine the illogic which often lies behind the facade of logic which parents present and which the adolescent is expected to accept. We also wish to give young people certain guidelines and clarifications about their parents, the better to understand the terrors, frustrations and disappointments that parents struggle with, so that their children may view them in a more sympathetic light and have some better feelings towards their parents.

Yet the concept of this book is surprisingly novel. While there seems to be no end of books written for and about adolescents, little time and space have been devoted to looking at the question of parental behavior in the life of the adolescent. Though we all know better, when we talk about adolescent turmoil and inconstancy, we tend to minimize the parts that parents play. It is easier, and perhaps self-serving, for adults talking and writing about adolescents to portray the erratic and stormy nature of these years as solely expressive of a young person's moves toward maturity and independence and to ignore the ways that parents can impede growth and confuse their children. Or, it may be more comfortable—when looking at parental indiscretions with their children—to conclude that the parents, while perhaps overreacting, are nonetheless *reacting* to their offspring's provocative behavior rather than, as we intend to illustrate, often themselves being the prime initiator of the adolescent's provocative behavior.

It is assumed that parenting is as easy a happening as breathing or falling asleep, and that one becomes a parent naturally and spontaneously and joyfully because one has once been a child and has had parents. We believe, however, that parenting is extraordinarily hard work, and that it does not come naturally to most of us: not only because of the complex mechanics involved, but because we, as adults and parents, struggle with the hidden residues of our own adolescence.

While the book is written primarily for the young, we suggest that parents may find some value in it. Our intent is, through mutual understanding, to ease and aid *families* during the formative years of their young.

Introduction

WELCOME TO THE CLUB
(WE'RE ALL IN IT TOGETHER)

Let's get it straight right at the start. We're going to take a long, hard look at the other side of the struggle that goes on during a person's adolescence. That is, we're going to look at your parents—and even your parents' parents. We're going to describe *why they think the way they think,* what it is they feel, what it is they believe in, *why they do what they do* and, ultimately, what irrationality lies behind their mask of rationality.

We don't have it in for parents. We're parents ourselves and, by and large, we like being parents. We've gone through (HAR) and are going through (LDT) many of the struggles we'll be describing in this book. We believe the struggle is necessary and can be worthwhile—for both adolescent and parent. And that's our point. It's not a one-sided struggle—it's not simply that adolescents are experiencing psychological and physical growth pains that makes them act the way they do. And it's not simply that parents have to grin and bear it and try to provide whatever support and discipline and advice they can during this "difficult period." But this period is also about the hang-ups and biases and fears and conflicts that *parents* bring to it and often dump right on the heads of their kids—usually without acknowledging (if they even realize it) that they are dumping anything or behaving towards their kids in any but the most wholesome, parental manner.

A typical parent says, "Sure I get upset and angry. Sometimes my head gets bent out of shape with all the anger and insolence and crap my teenagers bombard me with. It's a wonder I don't react worse than I do...I can't wait till they grow up." Sounds pretty honest, doesn't it? The parent is open and candid and willing to admit that he or she sometimes goofs. Right?...Wrong. This "typical" parent has, in this self-righteous comment, just dumped everything back on the kid. In effect the parent says, "*You* make me feel what I feel. *You* are responsible—by your insolent and uncooperative ways, *you* force me to do the things I do and *you* bend my head out of shape." This parent places the burden of blame for his own unhappiness upon his child. And he neglects to admit that he could bring into the conflict anything of his own—from his own considerable warehouse of problems—that could have caused it or, at least, blown it out of proportion. Further, the parent is really stating that his own frustrations and despairs—whether with himself, or his spouse, or with his job or with getting old or not having enough money or enough peace of mind—are off-limits, and have no relevance to the conflict with his adolescent son or daughter.

We say "bull" to this. We think that these issues are not only *not* off limits, but are where much of the real action takes place. And we intend to show how and why it's important, and how your better understanding of it will help you to deal better with it. Some of what we're talking about you probably knew all along, or maybe had an idea it was like this. But if you're like most young people, you probably felt it wasn't a safe subject to talk about with adults, especially your parents. We hope this book will legitimize these very important human issues and help both you and your parents to be able to think and talk about them in the open.

This brings us to another theme in our book. Did you ever have the crazy thought that your parents were born adults, that they *never* went through a phase of life called adolescence? They seem to forget what it was like for them when they were your age. Maybe, you think, they're reminded by you of all the weird and sexy and angry thoughts they had when they were young and now feel it's their duty to protect *you* from having. You're probably right, at least partially right, if you think this. Adults do tend to forget their own adolescent experiences. Like the mother who recently told us she couldn't understand why her daughter seemed resentful or sullen and moody and occasionally confronted her parents. She stated that, as far as she remembered, she had *never* been like this in her adolescence and certainly had never confronted *her* parents! (We think she's either forgotten a lot of inner turmoil or during her adolescence was studying to become a saint.)

As we said, adults do tend to forget their own past: *you, now in transit through what they went through twenty or thirty years ago, remind them of their past and make them feel uncomfortable.* We'll be talking a lot about forgetting and the consequences for them as well as for you of forgetting. And also what you can do about it.

One last point before we get started. Your parents and their generation aren't the first to forget their own past or to place almost the whole burden of adolescence on adolescents. Every generation seems to focus primarily on the young as having the problems, and on the elders as having to cope with those problems. And every generation tends to worry and be concerned about the next not fulfilling its responsibilities and letting the world go to "rack and ruin."

6

We thought you might be interested in what a well-known commentator had to say about the young a few generations ago:

> The young are in character prone to desire and ready to carry any desire they have formed into action. Of bodily desires it is the sexual to which they are most disposed to give way, and in regard to sexual desire they exercise no self-restraint. They are changeful too, and fickle in their desires, which are as transitory as they are vehement; for their wishes are keen without being permanent, like a sick man's fits of hunger and thirst. They are passionate, irascible, and apt to be carried away by their impulses. They are the slaves, too, of their passion, as their ambition prevents their ever brooking a slight and renders them indignant at the mere idea of enduring an injury. And while they are fond of honor, they are fonder still of victory; for superiority is the object of youthful desire, and victory is a species of superiority. Again, they are fonder both of honor and of victory than of money, the reason why they care so little for money being that they have never yet had experience of want...If the young commit a fault, it is always on the side of excess and exaggeration...for they carry everything too far, whether it be their love or hatred or anything else. They regard themselves as omniscient and are positive in their assertions; this is, in fact, the reason of their carrying everything too far. Also their offenses take the line of insolence and not of meanness. They are compassionate from supposing all people to be virtuous, or at least better than they really are; for as they estimate their neighbors by their own guilelessness, they regard the evils which befall them as undeserved, facetiousness being disciplined insolence.

The commentator's name was Aristotle. He wrote this around 2300 years ago. Now let's get on with the book.

Part I

WE'RE ALL DEPENDENT
(IT ALL DEPENDS
ON WHO DEPENDS ON WHOM)

Just when you think you're not a kid anymore, and just when you think you're starting to get someplace—you're getting to be a man or a woman—then you can be sure your parents will tell you that "they pay the bills" and "they make the decisions," and if you don't believe them you can ask *their* parents.

1

What This Book
Is All About

There are two ways of looking at things: the way you do, and the way your parents do. This may not seem like a major discovery; but actually there aren't many people who understand *why parents think the way they do.* In fact, so few people understand parents that it seemed to us that it was about time someone wrote about it.

What we're going to tell you about in this book is how parents get to think the way they do. Before we go any further, however, there are a few erroneous beliefs that must be discarded:

1) There is a secret school that prospective parents go to before their child is born that teaches them how to be unreasonable and how to mess up your life. This is not true. While some parents do attend classes on how to deliver a baby by natural childbirth and also how to care for the newborn, they are not instructed in these classes on how to mess up the lives of their children. (You doubtless consider that they seem to have had sufficient natural talent for it already.)

2) The double ring ceremony, resulting in your father and mother both wearing wedding bands on the third finger, left hand, puts them under the control of a mad scientist who hates children. False. This belief is the result of watching too many science fiction movies. (In the first

place, not all parents wear wedding rings. In the second place, with parents like these, who needs a mad scientist?)

3) As soon as a baby is conceived, an enzyme is released into the bloodstream of both mother and father which makes them forget what it's like to be a kid. Also false. (No such enzyme has been identified, which leaves us wondering just what it is that does make some parents forget what it's like to be a kid.)

Now we've said the magic word. It's not "enzyme," it's not "parents," and it's not "kid." No; the magic word is *forget.* And that's what this book is mostly going to be about: how come so many parents forget, what it really means to forget; what gets forgotten; and how people can try to remember....or not to forget.

The first thing we want to do is establish the fact that **parents were once adolescents themselves.** In one sense you already agree with this, and we can imagine some of you saying (not too kindly) "They're *still* adolescents!" In another sense, it's not too difficult to reach the logical conclusion that they must have passed through adolescence for them to have become adults, but knowing that it must be true doesn't necessarily make it any more believable. A third way of looking at it is to maintain obstinately that they must have passed directly from childhood into adulthood, without ever having known the joys and sorrows of the best (or worst) part of being alive.

Since we don't know how much of or what kind of adolescence your particular parents had, the best we can do is to say that they had *some* kind of adolescence, even though to listen to them you might never believe it.

We've just said the second magic word: *listen*. **We want you to listen to your parents, to hear what they have to say, to try to understand the source of their communications. Parents function in a number of roles, and everything they say is coming from somewhere.** In the next few chapters we will point out that they have various *role definitions*, and it is in these roles that their behaviors originate.

One of the sources of things your parents say is simply their job as parents: official statements from their official position as executives or as administrators for the family. In theory there should be nothing wrong with this. Ideally, when your parents talk like this they are being realistic, telling themselves and you about the actual state of affairs, as when they say, "We can't afford a new car this year." Sometimes these statements aren't absolutely true, but they're close enough. For example, maybe they could afford a new car this year, but it's more important to put a new roof on the house. They're entitled to make decisions like that.

But sometimes you think they're putting something over on you, and sometimes you think they're just being arbitrary, or pulling rank, or just talking out of their position of authority. Well, we all do that sometimes. Sometimes kids say things just because they're kids and because they have to make policy statements as if there were an International Union of Adolescents. Perhaps that's something we all have to watch out for, regardless of how old we are, because it is very difficult to keep from using what power you have; most people don't even try.

Another source of statements parents make is their identification with their socioeconomic status, or with The System. Most adults seem to be mostly satisfied with the system, because it seems to work out for them. At the same time most adults seem to have a lot of complaints about the system, because there's a lot of it that doesn't seem right or fair. But since it either works well for them (or they think it could work well for them if they were able to make the right moves), it follows that very few adults are revolutionaries. Despite their criticism of The System, they don't want to throw it over.

After all, parents have everything invested in The System. And "invested" here doesn't just mean money, because their whole *life* is invested in the system. Mostly, adults have had to do something they call "struggle" to attain whatever security they have, whether it's a lot of security or just a little. If they threw it up they wouldn't have anything, and they'd have to go all the way back to GO, but it might be too late to try to come around again, so they tend to stay with what they have.

There might have been a time when they could have thrown it all up and gone some other way, but after they got married and after you or your brother or sister were born, it began to seem too late to look for an alternative lifestyle, so they hung on to what they had, whatever it happened to be. And once a person gets into something, especially if there's no place else to go, they not only stay there, but often they begin to act as though *that's all there is.*

It may sound to you like an unreal, freaked-out state to be in, to act like one way of being is all there is when you know there are other ways of being. It may seem that growing up is like being hypnotized—like hearing someone repeat, "You will head straight for the top, you will not stop and smoke along the way," and you could also think of it as getting a shot that immunizes you against alternative lifestyles.

Actually there is something weird about being an adult, just as it's weird being a kid. When you're a kid it's weird because you know that somewhere in you there's a future adult which is you! and when you're an adult there's still an incompletely settled kid in you that you don't know is there—like a house that doesn't know it's haunted.

But the adult goes along all right, even with *you* having been born, until something happens—in your life or in your parent's life—and then what was merely weird becomes frightening and sometimes terrifying. To all of you.

In the next two chapters we will give some examples of weird and frightening disagreements which arise between adolescent children and their parents. The examples are not unusual; you may have experienced them or very similar situations yourself, and you can doubtless come up with a number of anecdotes out of your own life. In these examples there is expressed an adolescent's point of view and also a parent's point of view. Obviously, parent and adolescent are coming from two different places, because *they are both dealing with the same sets of facts, yet they reach different conclusions, and each is convinced that he (she) is right and that the other is wrong!* The young person who wants to go skiing with friends has no doubt that this is the correct and appropriate thing to do; in the same way, the parents are quite convinced that their child is wrong, and that she (he) should be going to her grandparents' party. So what we have here is a state of *conflict*. Not so much a conflict about the facts (although there does seem to be some misunderstanding), so much as a conflict of *interpretation*. And of course, how someone interprets a set of facts depends on where he's coming from: on his *frame of reference*, on his *system of values*.

In subsequent chapters we will consider more about the nature of the conflicts between adolescent and parent. We will see that the adolescent has a natural set of feelings about life, and wants to act on those feelings. The parent, however, feels obliged to redirect the adolescent's thinking, based on his own interpretation of the way society operates. In so doing, the parent seems to need to have the last word and the final decision. The parent seems to feel it necessary to be omniscient and omnipotent. He or she isn't, of course, but for several reasons has come to act that way. The parent tries to be right about matters of *fact*, whether it was Babe Ruth's batting average, or what Baby Ruth candy bars will do to your teeth, or the size of the Gross National Product last year. The parent also tries to speak with assurance on what are obviously matters of *belief*, such as religion or politics, and will try to convince the adolescent of the correctness of parental attitudes about matters of faith, morality, social and economic behavior, and also about proper sexual conduct.

Parents, of course, have been around longer, and they have had more experiences than their children of any age, and they are convinced that it is necessary for them to educate their children about subjects that are not necessarily taught in school, that is, how one actually goes about the business of living. Yet, in so doing, and with the best of intentions, the lessons that the parent tries to teach may be replete with error. One source of these errors is situational. As we will see later, part of the difficulty lies in the nature of communication itself, while another part of this difficulty lies in the very fact of being a parent: in the adult condition. This too breaks down into two parts, for the adult condition is partly composed of the circumstances surrounding the need to work and earn a living, and partly of the circumstances surrounding the state of being married. The parent's dilemma is that he is constantly confronted with things he can't control: the nature of communication, his (her) job, his (her) spouse. Certainly he should be able to control his own kids! But, lo and behold, he can't control them either!

We shall see that a major reason for the adult's being out of touch with his adolescent children is that he has lost contact with his own adolescence, and that this may be brought back to him with a very rude jolt, sometimes with disastrous consequences.

Finally, we will exhort you to **try to understand how your parents got that way and to realize that, while some of the changes which occur as you move into adult life are inevitable,** *there are others that you may be able to do something about.* **This will be of considerable benefit to you and to your children. In the meantime, you can certainly afford to** *listen* **to what your parents are saying, and perhaps this book can help you to understand them a little better.**

2

That Old Dependency

It seemed like forever until you had everything together for a skiing weekend. As a junior in high school you had to find time when there were no exams coming up on Monday, no term papers to write, no major school activity where you positively had to show, you had the good snow, the right weather, the money for the trip, and most of all, the right people. Especially one guy. A guy you wanted to get away with. You had been thinking about this all the time. Not just the skiing, but being with him after your final run for the day. Talking, looking, being close.

So you told your folks, casually, that you had worked it out with some of the kids that you would all leave together Friday after school and you'd be back reasonably early Sunday evening.

Your father just mumbled something, and that was half the battle won. Now it was simply a matter of slipping it past Mother, which shouldn't be too hard because you were planning healthy outdoor activity which would be good for your skin and for your figure and it would tone up your muscles. And all this good health would help your mind so that you would do even better work in school next week. Right? Wrong.

"Next weekend," repeated your mother, then suddenly she screamed at you, "Next weekend! Next weekend is your grandmother and grandfather's fortieth wedding anniversary! Don't you realize that I've been working on this for the past three months? Where have you been? Don't you know what goes on in this house?"

You felt as though you had been shot. Why did *you* have to be at the party? you argued. What was so important about a fortieth wedding anniversary? A *fiftieth* would be really something and you'd be there for that, but what was so great about a *fortieth*? Just another party. You talked fast.

Then you went into all the planning you'd had to do to get this weekend arranged, how it was probably the only weekend all winter when you could get the gang together, and what a great thing it would be, and what a great time you'd have. Naturally you said nothing about the guy you wanted to be with; how could parents possibly understand a thing like that?

But regardless of what they could or couldn't understand, your weekend was sabotaged. You were going to the family party and that's all there was to it. Period. End of discussion. ("Not another word out of you, you're not too big to be smacked.") The only thing you'd ever really wanted was snatched away from you. (Forty years your grandparents had been together; you couldn't swing one lousy little weekend!)

But you were fighting a losing battle. The only way you could get to go was simply to take off and go, and let whateve happened happen. You could only think of that guy— skiing wasn't even in it—and how you wanted to be with him, and you were almost ready to take the consequences, whatever they might be. But you were only seventeen, and it was still pretty frightening to be in total defiance of your family. They had never thrown you out of the house, but you had never blatantly disobeyed them either, and there was no telling what they might do. Your father might beat the hell out of you, but then—you almost grinned—you could get him for child abuse! You were surprised to find yourself feeling a little better at the thought.

But what would you tell your friends? You were the one who had set this thing up, and if you suddenly dropped out, how would that look! As you felt weak and helpless and ashamed toward your friends you got angrier and angrier at your mother. What an absolutely impossible situation she was putting you in! What CRUD*!

This was all because you were a kid in their eyes, a mere child, one of those "adolescents," someone big enough and smart enough to know how to run their own life, but not old enough to get away with it. If you were a child it would be a different matter, but—and you thought of your guy— you certainly didn't feel like a child, and...you wouldn't feel like a child to him. You bristle with the frustration that comes from someone else having such control over you. And probably you hunger for the day when you'll be on your own and able to call your own shots.

Quite right: you were a second-class citizen, discriminated against as a member of a minority group. You were being treated like a slave, like a criminal.

There is a certain kind of criminal who is known as a *status offender*. He has committed a crime simply because of who he is or what he is. For example, let's suppose that you're an alien, and suddenly the word is out that all aliens have to register. In every post office there's a sign saying "All Aliens Must Register," and the message is in the newspapers and repeated on radio and on television. If you don't register, you're automatically a criminal. If you hadn't been an alien you wouldn't have had to register; therefore your offense is an offense simply because of your status as an alien.

---

*CRUD—Crises Recurring Under Dependency

There is a reasonable parallel in your situation. While the law in most states now recognizes the rights of minors when it comes to legal matters, such laws don't, for the most part, influence what goes on within your home. And in the home the adolescent *is* in a dependent position and has at best only partial control over his own life and actions.

So there is a certain resemblance between the status offense situation out in the world and the situation of the adolescent at home. To a certain extent you're in trouble just because you're there, and sometimes you may get to feel that your very presence is a crime against humanity, and you may feel like saying things like "Hang me," or "Kill me," or "Throw me out; I'm no good." That's not necessarily because of anything you've done, but simply because of your status in the household: although you may be big enough and possibly capable enough to do many of the things an adult does, you're nevertheless still in a dependent situation.

Now this business of being dependent is a very tricky thing and it operates very subtly. Sometimes a person feels dependent when he isn't, and sometimes he may not feel dependent when he is, and sometimes someone else may feel he's dependent on them, or not dependent on them, and he may feel just the opposite. So let's be clear that what we're talking about here may not be the way you feel in your head, but it's about your *status*, which is the way the law or society, including the Internal Revenue Service, looks at it. *If you're under age you're a dependent, and your parents have all kinds of legal rights, including the right to claim a deduction for you on their income tax, even if you're of age, provided they're paying for at least half of your upkeep.*

Aha, you say, it all comes down to money. In a way it

does, but if you were earning a million dollars a year as a rock star you'd still have the status of a dependent. Even if you felt you could leave home and run your own life and didn't need anyone to make your decisions for you it wouldn't make any difference, because the law sees you as a dependent, and if you ran away you'd be classed as a runaway, which is again a kind of status offender.

So when you put it all together it turns out that in a way, you're stuck. But if you look at this just a little further you'll find that your parents are also stuck.

Further, there is a weird feeling to your situation, as far as your parents are concerned. Your presence there causes vibrations with something within them, so that in addition to being yourself, you're also part of a memory, of a dream.

Now let's look at where your mother is in this situation. In doing this we will start at the top, looking first at the more obvious, perhaps more superficial aspects of the situation and not immediately jump to the conclusion that your mother is jealous of you and would herself like to be off skiing (which might be true, but also might not).

What we do have to accept is that your mother has been deeply involved in her parents' anniversary party for several months. It is most likely that she'd at least mentioned it to you, but even if she hadn't it is reasonable to believe that she assumed that she had and that she took it for granted that you would be at the affair. Accordingly she had created an expectation that you would be there along with the rest of the family, and she was therefore shocked to hear that you had made other plans. That is to say, she really was shocked, and it wasn't just a piece of playacting.

You may feel that she had no right to be shocked because you didn't know about the party, but from her point of view it was most natural, even inevitable, that she feel shocked. Further, there is *no way* for you to convince her that you didn't know about it.

The next point is that, from her position, it is strictly a matter of course that you would be there. Part A to this point is that she believes you would want to be there, to honor and celebrate with your grandparents and the rest of the family. (Actually, you would be bored stiff because there's no one your own age, no one you know.)

Part B is that even if you didn't want to be there, you'd have to come anyway because it was right for you to be there and it was expected of you (not just expected by her, but by "everybody"). So where do you come off having something else to do or somewhere else to go? The fact that you would want to go skiing, that you'd arranged something that wasn't easy to accomplish, that you'd been looking forward to it, that you wanted to be with your friends (for whatever reasons) would cut absolutely no ice with her. Indeed she would be horrified to think that you cared so little for your family that you would even *dream* of being with anyone else! ("Do you hate your family so much that you won't spend one day with them?" Of course you don't hate your family. Most of the time you at least tolerate them, sometimes you find them almost pleasant. You actually love your grandmother. So why is Mother reacting so strongly and being so hateful toward you?)

Your mother, quite understandably, is concerned with the issues of *duty, responsibility,* and *family loyalty.* These principles, guaranteed to set your teeth on edge and to upset your gut so much you wouldn't even be able to digest yogurt, are the prime weapons of parents against their offspring. Even if these principles as arguments make no logical sense to you, they nevertheless can produce feelings of fear (without your knowing what you're afraid of) and guilt (without your being quite sure what it is you've done).

1) *Duty,* in brief, means that you have to do what your parents tell you to do simply because your parents are your superior officers: certainly older, presumably wiser, and obviously with more pull or much more power than you.

2) *Responsibility* means that because we're here on this earth, each of us has the job of holding part of the universe (or the family, whichever is larger) together, like Atlas holding the world on his shoulders. In family language this means that if you don't go to the party the entire family will be smitten by plague.

"Duty" and "Responsibility" are standards, classics; both are righteous and unassailable, guaranteed never to fail as ammunition in a parental war of moral persuasion. Every generation uses them; maybe yours will too. True they may not win many battles, but they do inflict wounds of guilt and seething resentment. And they are potent, noxious, and effective smokescreens that cover and hide the real issues at stake.

3) *Family loyalty* may have more practical implications for you. After all, your mother will say, "Blood is thicker than water," and—who are your real friends if not your family? Where will your skiing friends be, she will ask, after the snow melts? And while you're working on that one, she may hit you with, "Who will send you to college, your skiing friends?" (That last one may be a little unfair, but who's fair in love and war?)

Fortunately, good old Dad is there to resolve the situation. The party isn't until Saturday night, so you can still get in a whole day of skiing and be back in time to dance the Anniversary Waltz, or hustle, or something.

Now let's look at this a little deeper. Your mother is still very much caught up in her own feelings of duty, responsibility and family loyalty, and she is deeply hurt that you don't seem to have the same kind of feelings for her that she has toward her own parents. Further, she has a *need* for you to continue to be dependent on your family. Her own feelings of security as a parent (and as a child!) are *threatened* by your readiness to go off and do things on your own. Both of your parents are probably hurt that you don't *need* to be with them as you once did; that you don't *need* to rely on them; *need* to wait for them, hang on them, be hugged by them, have your hand held by them as you once did. As much as a part of you wants to lessen this sense of dependency upon them and as much as a part of them encourages your growing and maturing, so another more vulnerable, more fragile, and usually less obvious part of them (as perhaps a part of you) wishes to hang onto that dependency and *needs* that dependency, that sense of need coming from you.

Your needing them less is felt as and comes out as *disloyalty*. Your parents may well feel betrayed, rejected, abandoned. You prefer someone over them, someone whom they are internally compelled to devalue no matter how fine he or she may be. (You do seem to be indifferent to your parents and indeed most likely are. For quite naturally, your interests often now are elsewhere. But maybe, secretly, you also enjoy provoking them by your appearance of unconcern, of indifference towards them.)

While a few parents might be able openly and directly to acknowledge these hurt feelings to themselves and their children, your parents may be unable to do so. Instead they may respond in roundabout, indirect ways, trying to insist on their control, trying to reestablish lines of authority by playing on your sense of guilt and by expressing anger and by moralizing. There is even more than a small chance that Mom is aware of your emerging (or emerged) sexuality, and she would still like to keep you young and pure and childlike. There may or may not be some envy of your vigorous youthfulness, but the probability is that your mother is a long way from considering herself over the hill.

One other thing that might be mentioned here is the strong bond between mothers and daughters. She actually wants you to be with her at this time, not just to teach you how to become a woman, but because she has actual pleasure in your company.

This touches on two of the central themes we are exploring in this book:
  1. The theme of your parents' need for control.
  2. The theme of your parents' own adolescence.

In describing the typical situation of a parent exercising control over a child, we are mindful of the hidden meanings and many factors involved in "control." Obviously, with control goes power, strength, will and dominance. In the extreme, one person rules the life of another; the parent rules the child. And the child is forced to be compliant, has to be submissive. Or rebellious. But it is not that simple or clear-cut. For there are less obvious aspects of control, deep within your parents, which play a part in how they act, sometimes even against their own better judgment. Assuming that your parents are not power-hungry—as most parents are not—then some needs within them, some major discontents and unfulfillments in their lives, are important factors in their doing what they sometimes do with their children.

And what about your parents' own adolescence? While they most certainly have excellent recall of details of their teenage years—how they got on with their parents and their peers, how they did in school, what kind of scrapes they got into, what kind of exciting times they had, what their first love was like—they have lost touch, most likely, with some elemental and vital part of their emotional experience in that crucial period of life. For the paradox is that, as one leaves the home and one moves into maturity, one tends to forget or lose sight of that inexpressible spirit which characterized the struggle of becoming an adult. And this makes them seem not able to understand you and your similar predicament.

In the illustration we have been using, the conflict between mother and adolescent over going or not going to the grandparents' anniversary party, there is another, ironic twist. For your mother is vibrating to the themes of control and her own buried youth with her own mother. She is caught in the middle; that is, while she is your mother—grown up, independent, relatively mature and responsible, used to making decisions—she is, at the same time *your grandmother's daughter* and as such she carries within her the remnants of her own childhood and adolescence... being dependent, relatively immature, seeming to lack responsibility. Your mother may need to have you present at the party as a sign of loyalty and duty to her mother. She may even fear her own mother's criticism, real or imagined, and *your not being present may make her feel that she is deficient both as a mother and as a daughter. So when your mother lectures you about duty*

*and responsibility she may actually, secretly, be asking you
for help, but asking for it in a way that is difficult for you to
perceive, let alone respond to.*

Now it begins to get difficult. When it's just a matter of
words, we can say very easily to each other that we understand that our parents were, and still are, their parents' children, and that to some extent our parents still
feel like their parents' children. But when we look at parents and see them as mature and wise and powerful, it's
hard to realize that they may actually feel uncertain and
insecure and intimidated by their own parents, or by their
parents' ideas that they have taken into themselves. It's
only when we see our parents behaving timidly, or irration-
ally, or inconsistently, that we get a sense of some mysterious force operating in them. And when we feel that
they aren't behaving the way we think our parents
should, then *we* feel puzzled and insecure, and sometimes frightened and even discouraged or depressed.
Why can't they understand, we wonder, and we feel
hopelessly frustrated that we can't get through to them.

**The problem isn't that we can't get through to them.
The problem is that we get through too well, and stir up
old feelings and confusions in them, with the result that,
instead of their becoming more understanding of us,
they actually, without knowing why, may end up feeling
resentful toward us. And that's how we all get into these
big hassles.**

3

You're Never Too Old

Some of you may find Chapter 2 old hat, yesterday's newspaper. Maybe it applied to you a couple of years ago, but no longer. You resolved the conflict with your parents and carved out the right to make your own decisions. Or maybe, you wise oracle, you never had that problem anyway, because your grandparents are dead or live in another city.

So what else is new, you say. You've got more important things to do. For instance, your freshman humanities paper on Camus and Kierkegaard. And finals are coming up. It's been an intense and exciting fall semester, this first year away at college. You didn't study as consistently as you might have, but there were a lot more interesting things to do—socializing, athletics and so on. Anyway, you'll make up for it now by cramming, staying up all night to get the work done, the finals completed so you can get home for Christmas. You look forward to seeing all the old friends from high school, swapping stories with them—and you look forward to having a bit of nostalgia and old-fashioned good-time feelings with the family.

The family. You walk in the door absolutely beat from a week of finals and your dad says your hair's too long and cruddy. Your mom cries because you've got a suggestion of a beard and little sister asks whether you've brought any good pot...right in front of them! (She doesn't have any better sense than she had four months ago.) And boy, does that start it. Right at the front door and you haven't even gotten your coat off!

"You can do whatever you want when you're away from here, but I'll have no drugs in my house," says Mom.

"I back her 200 percent on that," says Dad. "If you've got any junk on you, get rid of it right now before you come in any further."

Well, you get through that one, and get your stuff up to your room, which looks good and neat and all sparkled up, but not right. All the funkiness is missing, the casual sloppiness, the posters, the notes to yourself pinned to the door. Oh well, Mom finally did what she always threatened to do last year, but couldn't because you wouldn't let her. She cleaned your room. That's cool. Maybe a little nap before dinner. The old bed feels the same. And off you go.

When you awaken and come down to dinner, you see that Mom has that icy stare on her face, the one she reserves for when she's miffed and hurt. You ask what's wrong and, naturally, she tells you nothing's wrong. So you have a pleasant talk about what a glorious time you've been having, doing this and that, going here and there. Dad tries to sober the atmosphere a bit by inquiring about your grades and reminding you that you're at college to get an education, not to have a good time.

The phone rings. It's Jill ... You'll be right over ... You ask for the car tonight ... If no one else is using it, of course. And that's when you find out about Mom's icy stare.

"You've been home four hours and hardly had a civil word with us," she explodes. "The first thing you do is take a nap. Then you come to dinner and all you talk about is you and your college. You don't care about us.

You didn't have the courtesy to ask how Dad's been feeling, after all he's been through. No thought for me. And now you want to go out with your friends. What are we? A motel?"

Your plans seem to go awry. Maybe you've been too selfish and not considerate of your family. So you call up Jill, tell her something's come up, and you'll see her tomorrow night. You make amends by spending that night in the bosom of the family (instead of Jill's) and being very helpful around the house the next day.

Everything's set now for you and Jill to get together. "I hope you folks won't mind too much if I spend some time with Jill tonight. It's been a long time since we've seen each other and we've got a lot to talk about."

"Of course not," they respond, picking up on your air of cordiality and politeness. "We think that's just fine. And we have plans ourselves with the Frobishers...But

  —Where are you going?
  —Who are you going to be with?
  —What time will you be in?

Their questions hit you right in the solar plexus. You've grown considerably in the last four months and have a taste of the freedom you never want to lose. You've not had to answer to anyone but yourself about where you've gone and what you've done. But you don't want to antagonize your parents, so you say, "We don't know exactly what we'll be doing. We may see if we can round up some of the gang or find out if there's a party anywhere. And I don't know what time I'll be in. So don't wait up for me."

"Just a minute, son," says Dad. "That sounds awfully vague to me. Mom and I don't want you cruising around the countryside, especially during these holiday times when there are so many drunk drivers on the road...And I don't want you smoking any pot...And I want you home by 1:00 A.M."

In the argument that follows you are likely to state your position as follows: Since being away at college, you've been more or less on your own. You've managed your affairs reasonably well and have set your own hours. You don't see why, when you come home to visit, that you have to be treated like a child having to tell your parents where you're going, what you're doing, and abide by a curfew.

Your parents' argument is equally clear: They certainly realize they have no say in how you conduct your life when you're away from home. And they can in no way control what you do or don't do. But when you are home, they will have some input into your actions and will ask you to abide by the rules of their home. As a further example, they cite that while they do not condone premarital sex, if you were having a sexual relationship with a woman, they could do nothing to prevent it. But if you brought the woman home you would have to subscribe to their moral code and not have sexual relations within the house.

Both of your arguments are crystal clear. And in conflict. Yours seem reasonable to you, theirs to them. But they are miles apart and you are at an impasse. Add to this that it is most likely that they had similar conflicts with their parents when they were your age. When they returned home from college they asked for the same freedoms you are asking for and were denied them in similar fashion. Yet they—having once been where you are now, and having once felt the same feelings of frustration and vexation toward their parents as you feel toward them—react to you in a similar manner to the way their parents reacted to them. You would think that they would have profited from their own experience and be more "reasonable" with you!

This is simply not the case—not because they forget they were once in your shoes (they probably remember all too well), but because they must carry out the functions of their *role definition*. They were told, as they probably tell you, that "You will understand when *you* are a parent." The role definition of a parent is:

(1) to be responsible for others
(2) to set limits for others
(3) to hang on.

Your role definition, as you seek emancipation for yourself, is:

(1) to learn to be responsible for yourself
(2) to find what your own limits are
(3) to let go.

These definitions have to do with the expectations and demands of an assigned role. You see this most clearly when people are in transition from one role to another. For instance, young marrieds will put aside their motorcycles over a period of time, stop going to nightclubs, dress differently and develop different attitudes toward money. They will become more conservative and protective in their attitude and actions as they shift from one role to another. You also see role definition differences in people's dress and manners. An example would be a college professor versus a banker. Both, for argument's sake, come from the same background; both are equally well educated. Yet one dresses differently from the other, significantly, and his style of relating to others is also different.

So now your parents' reality is the reality of being a parent, of assuming and carrying out what is expected of them as parents, as persons whose duties are to provide safeguards and limits for their children. It makes no difference that you probably don't need either safeguards or limits at this time in your life. For the reality of role definition, the reality of your parents as parents, often has little to do with your own reality.

Add to this, of course, the fact that parents like to—need to—hang on to you. There's always something more to be done, some further guidance in living, some more polishing of your character and responsibilities, something unfinished. Though it is done in the spirit of giving and often with the sigh of weariness or the crackle of irritation, it is, in reality, done because *the parent needs you more than you need him or her at this time.* By definition, *a parent needs a child in order to be a parent.* A parent, with the child gone, must shift in role definition of himself, must make major changes in his or her identity, must find other avenues of self-fulfillment and purpose. Mothers, especially those whose interests have been focused on the home and on child-rearing, suffer from a sadness, a depression that has been called the "empty nest syndrome." *The anticipation of emptiness, of losing a sense of purpose and meaning, evokes tremendous anxiety within the individual. And it often comes out as a wanting to hang on—to* "smother."

So you're never too old for your parents to want to keep you young.

Part II

CONFLICT OF VALUES
(IN CASE OF A TIE,
GUESS WHO WINS!)

Once upon a time long ago your parents seemed to know everything, and you knew nothing. Later you thought you knew everything and your parents nothing. But knowing everything isn't everything; sometimes it isn't anything.

4

The Mask Of Omniscience (Father/Mother Knows Best)

How far back can you remember? Can you remember what it was like to be three or four years old? Maybe you can remember back to when you were two, or even farther back than that. Can you remember how powerful your parents seemed when you were little? Your father could swoop you up in his arms and hold you high in the air where you would flap your arms and legs, happy and terrified, squealing in delight and fear, and then he would whirl you down and around in a thrilling, dizzying roller-coaster ride. When your parents were happy they could make you happy just being with you, and when they were upset or angry or frightened you would have nowhere to go to escape the feeling of emptiness and isolation and hopelessness that their feelings produced in you. What enormous power they had over your emotions!

And what power they had over your mind, over your understanding and imagination! They knew the explanation of all things. They knew why flowers flower and why the sun comes up and where it goes after it sets. They knew the magic of words and numbers, how to combine words into sentences and numbers into sums and products. And they had the power to protect you: to make pain go away and to banish ghosts and monsters from your room. Now there's a strange paradox here for your parents. They probably did not fully appreciate the tremendous impact they had on you as a kid, this power to make you either blissfully happy and content, or profoundly sad and frightened. Yet at the same time, they enjoyed and felt good about this power they had over you. It was something they had never experienced before. They had never felt so much in command, nor as loving and giving as they could be with you. These feelings would give them personal meaning, would enhance their self-esteem, and bring out the most loving part of them.

As you grew older, their powers seemed to diminish. Their explanation of how things work often became a little less than satisfying, and frequently did not quite agree with what you learned from your science teachers. And something seemed to be happening to your parents' ability to conjure up that old black magic: when things went wrong in your life there often didn't seem to be anything that they could kiss and make better. When you suffered from feelings of insecurity about your looks or your athletic abilities or your social skills, somehow their reassurances didn't compensate for your not having made the team or for not going out with that guy or girl you wanted. And as you got jobs and had some money of your own, their ideas on how much you should save and what you should spend it on didn't seem to fit in very well with the current scene.

As a matter of fact, your parents' views on how the world works lately seemed to be slipping out of date. They really didn't have a good idea of the way life was changing all around them.

Nevertheless they continued to tell you what was what, how things should be done, their views on music, movies,

politics, clothes, sex, food, money, morality, sports, education, work, sleep, drugs, health, cars, and a lot of other
things, some of which you couldn't always give a name
to. Naturally, no one could be expected to know a lot
about so many things—though your dad did know a lot
about automobiles and your mother was an awfully good
cook. Doubtless they knew a lot of things that had to do
with the other, hidden side of their life, but that didn't
seem to have anything to do with the things you were
doing. Your dad would put his hand on your shoulder,
look you squarely in the face, and say something like,
"Buy low, sell high," and that would throw him into a
chuckle, or a cackle, or a fit of laughter, and you would
kind of just look at him. And sometimes he would say
something like, "Don't take any wooden nickels."

Of course, when he would say things like that he may
have just been kidding around, or maybe not. You
couldn't tell. So you really didn't know how to react.

We have a hunch that your father was kidding when he
came out with these things, but that it was a special kind
of kidding that used to be called "kidding on the square."
That means that he meant what he said, but he was
saying it as a joke in order to protect himself in case it
didn't go over very well. He was, in fact, trying to tell you
something, but he no longer knew how to tell you.

It certainly isn't very hard to figure out that parents
very easily get into the habit of telling their children
about the world. Being big and important and all-know-
ing is hard to resist and extremely difficult to give up. It is
very easy for parents to keep telling themselves that their
children need their wisdom and instruction even after
their children are no longer children, and even after they

have experienced a hint that their advice and assistance is no longer welcome. They know, or at least they believe, that there will come a time when you will be glad to come to them for help, or at least that you are or will be reassured merely by their being there.

There is some sense to this, for it is reassuring to have your parents waiting in the wings in case you need them. But how many times have you wished that they would be content just to be there, and not to impose their ideas and values on you!

But it is hard for them to stay in reserve, just as it is hard for an athlete to sit on the bench while his teammates are out there on the court or on the field locked in combat. So they burst out with a statement, an action, an exclamation, and you call a technical foul as would a referee who sees that one team has too many players.

Why do they jump on the court when they're not needed? *Why do they intrude on your life? We think it has something to do with their felt loss of power, with their not being needed so much.* For in your adolescent years, as you hunger for independence and self-government, you are likely—quite naturally and normally—to realign your sights so as to devalue your parents. At many points during your adolescence you will undoubtedly have far less appreciation of them than is really their due. You may see them as unknowing, as ignorant, as backward, as rigidly conservative, as unappreciative of you in your budding maturity.

But they, how do they see you? How have they reacted to you as you have become more of an independent being, more able to stand on your own two feet? Probably their reaction has been mixed. Most parent reactions are mixed.

Certainly the obvious aspect of their reaction is positive.

They are happy for you, glad to see you emerge as a vital person, rejoicing in your triumphs, sorrowing in your failures, proud of you when you do well, angry when you don't do so well. And probably even secretly relieved. The more you emerge, the less the terrible and weighty burden on them becomes. For let's make no bones about it, the pressures of parenting—if one is at all concerned and thoughtful about parenting—are enormous. The worries in the middle of the night, the anguish and guilt over having been too harsh with you, the bewilderment and confusion of not knowing how to respond to problems you may have in thriving, the fears for you and the fears for them being good parents to you, all these are concerns of your parents. And they are, for the most part, well known to you; for parents, like most people, want to get credit and recognition for their hard work and sacrifice.

Yet there is another, more silent, less obvious side to your parents' mixed reaction to your maturation. And that is their reaction to their loss of control and power over you. *There is something terribly compelling in one being able to have as absolute a sense of power over another as the parent has over the small child.* At first bewildered, frightened by the awesome responsibility and not well prepared for it, the typical parent comes soon to like that sense of importance and centrality that he most likely has in no other area of his life, not even with his spouse. This power is seductive and addicting. Seldom, if ever, does he experience the awesome and idolizing riveting of attention upon him as he did with his small child when he walked into a room. Seldom does his love or anger evoke such an unequivocal and clear response from any adult. Seldom are his words weighed so honestly, so earnestly listened to. And in the adult world of compromise and disappointment, of failure and frustration, of conflict and disagreement, his relations with his child are, for him, a safe haven. Thus your adoration of him is as important for him, for his own needs, as it is for you.

So when you grow and need your parents less, they are liable secretly (perhaps even secretly from themselves) to resent you. They probably do not like this dark side of their reaction to you and will keep it out of their own consciousness altogether or will attempt to rationalize it in some way. When you choose not to listen to them or to form your own opinion, they may react as if you don't have the capability to judge for yourself. When you err in doing something or forget to do something (like taking out the garbage) or choose not to do something, they may pounce on this as a cardinal sign of your irresponsibility and immaturity and thus still have need to acknowledge your dependence upon them.

Now this is all fairly obvious to someone who is observing the scene, but it is far from obvious while it is going on. Indeed it often looks as though there is no outside world that you're learning to deal with, but that the universe consists exclusively of you and your parents, locked in a deadly power struggle. We sit here calmly and say that, yes, the adolescent is struggling to gain his independence in living in the community, and that, yes, your parents are reluctant to give up their power over you and are also unsure if you're ready to handle your own life decisions. But from where you are it's as though you and your parents are pushing and jarring each other like opposing linemen, or that you're trying to run with the ball and they're clawing at you and clinging to your jersey. Sometimes it's worse than that, and you may think they're trying to destroy you, while you wish they would just go away or die. (Not necessarily painfully, but once and for all.)

It doesn't make much difference who started the adversary situation, especially since no one really meant to turn it into a hassle. It's possible that you have been maturing faster than your parents could recognize, so that their instructions have kept coming somewhat after they're no longer needed; it's equally possible that you've been pressing unrealistically to emancipate yourself from parental control. But *once it becomes an out-and-out power struggle, there's no such thing as "right," because everyone's wrong:* the basic issue of your learning to deal with life gets lost in the babel of self-assertive pronouncements.

The assumption of maturity must be accomplished rhythmically, as when you're learning to use a manual gearshift: one foot has to come up as the other goes down. Otherwise the vehicle gets stalled or its gears get ground. In family life there aren't many automatic transmissions, especially on the road to becoming an adult.

You really have to concentrate on what it is that you're trying to do with your life, or what goal you're trying to reach and *how to reach it;* otherwise, with the best of intentions, your parents will call you incompetent, and your progress is impeded. In actuality they are in a very tough situation. Even if they finally want to give up their power, they're afraid of turning you loose too soon, so if you don't give them a very good clue as to where you're at—of just how mature you are in dealing with situations (which means dealing with people)—the hassles are very close to inevitable.

5

The Preservation Of Western Civilization (Let's Not Spoil A Good Thing)

Sometimes you wonder, "Where did they ever get ideas like that!" Your parents tell you that it isn't healthy for you to drink or to smoke pot because it'll pickle your brain or wreck your chromosomes. Or they tell you that it's important to go right through school and get a job and marry and have kids and a house of your own. Or else they say that you should join a church or a synagogue or something because otherwise you might not go to Heaven. Or they say that you should participate in community activities as a junior grade Rotarian or Knight of Columbus, or future Moose or Elk or Shriner so you can get middle-aged and dance around in a fez. Or they tell you it's important to vote in the primary elections because that's how democracy works. Do parents really believe in all that?

It's hard to know what people really believe in. Grown-up people, adults, probably really believe in things like Walter Cronkite, aspirin, the Montreal Canadiens, *The Wall Street Journal*, Jack Nicklaus, and maybe the value of a good education. They'll tell you it's important to believe in God, the Federal Reserve Bank, germs, Congress and the White House and the Supreme Court, and General Motors. But you'll also hear grown-ups, parents, express their doubts that there is a God, criticize the policies of the Federal Reserve Bank, make light of the dangers of infection (or else overemphasize them), curse all three branches of government, and generally condemn big business. So it's not really too clear where people put their faith.

One thing is clear, and that is that *people of all ages believe in success, and they therefore tend to believe in what works and in people who are successful.* Of course parents and their adolescent children are not too likely to agree on what works and on who the real stars are: the same people don't usually believe in both Lawrence Welk and The Rolling Stones. Parents, of course, have been around longer than their children, and their stars have generally been around longer. It follows, then, that parents consider their stars to be the real and lasting stars, and that their kids' stars are just shooting stars and will burn themselves out.

All this doesn't just have to do with singers and groups and TV performers; it also has to do with organizations and institutions and political parties, churches, philosophies, systems of morality, and breakfast cereals. And the general principle is: what *we* belong to, what *we* believe in, the particular corn, oat, or wheat flakes that *we* eat, are the ones that have proven themselves over the years, and are accordingly the *right* things to participate in, worship, or brush your teeth with. Because, obviously, if they weren't the *best*, we wouldn't have anything to do with them, and they wouldn't have lasted!

So, here you are, a nice clean-cut Orthodox Methodist Jewish urban/suburban kid, and you've decided to become a Zen Buddhist. You're fed up with the materialism and the meaninglessness and purposelessness of the way your parents and their friends and neighbors live, and you want to get in touch with something that really gets down to where it's really at, to the essence of existence.

Your parents say, "You're *what*?" And, "You're *crazy*!" They ask you how you ever expect to get a job as a Zen Buddhist, where will you ever find anybody to marry you, and what will happen to your children? So you say that you won't have any children, that you'll be a monk, and your mother begins to cry because she'll never get to be a grandmother, at least not if it depends on you! This is kind of puzzling, because your mother is very concerned about looking her age, and also keeps telling you how awful and ungrateful children are, and how much better off one is without them.

Now you know that Zen Buddhism is not some kind of trivial nonsense, but is a serious religion based on simplicity, moral discipline, mental training and meditative introspection. It is a derivative of Buddhism, which is an older faith than Christianity; widely followed in India, China (at least before Mao), and Japan. And if you want to argue point for point, which never gets you anywhere anyway, it makes as much sense as any religion, especially because religions don't work through logic, but rather because they enable people, as Pascal said, to make the "leap of faith."

For all any of us knows, from the viewpoint of the logic of that Great Computer in the sky, Zen Buddhism makes as much sense as any other religion. Indeed your parents will agree that simplicity, moral discipline, mental training, and meditative introspection are very desirable attributes of any faith, and they will even point out to you that this is what the Quakers go in for in a big way, and some of their best friends are Quakers.

But the point is, who in the neighborhood is a Zen Buddhist? Even that neat architect, Tony Nakimura, goes to the Episcopal Church, and that should tell you something! Well, it does tell you something; it tells you that Tony Nakimura wants to be accepted as a JAASP (Japanese-American Anglo-Saxon Protestant), and that your parents obviously look with favor on anyone who recognizes at least approximately where it's at—that is, somewhere in the general vicinity of the Judeo-Christian ethic.

Because, after all, where do we live? On the southern slope of Mt. Everest or at 337 Maplewood Drive? Let's face it, kid! You're always talking about "where it's at"; OK then, 337 Maplewood Drive is where it's at. What are you doing, messing around with this Oriental stuff?

There seems to be some confusion here. Your interest in Zen Buddhism was on a high moral, intellectual, and emotional level. You thought you were trying to become the fine sensitive, spiritual person your parents and minister have always wanted you to become. But it turns out that what they really want is for you to worship at the church of *their* choice, to be in awe of what you're *supposed* to be in awe of, and get in touch with the truly eternal forces of the Universe not by any kind of direct spiritual contact, but by joining the *right* church, by paying your dues every year, and by appearing on the scene every week (and certainly on the Holy Days).

All this, of course, you label hypocrisy, just as your parents label you rebellious.

Isn't there some way to get this together? Well, perhaps, if we can figure out where you and your parents are, separately, coming from.

The odds are that your parents haven't ever tried to think this through. They grew up in their respective, respectable households and attended the church of *their* parents' choice, went to Sunday School, and learned some particular version of the eternal verities. While they may have learned that there are other versions of Creation and of the Deity, it is likely that they grew up thinking there was something slightly erroneous, or naive, or supersophisticated, or whifty, about other people's religions. If theirs is one of the oldest faiths, the chances are that they believe that the oldest is the best, and that all modifications have resulted in an inferior product. If, on the other hand, their sect is of more recent origin, they are proud to be among those who have finally got it all straight. In either case they doubtless see a direct progression from the origin of the Universe to the most recent sermon by their minister. In this progression they see the continuity of a firm moral thread that holds together the fabric of Western Civilization, which you, you young heretic, infidel, mischievous unbeliever, are threatening to snap with reckless abandon by your negativistic dabblings in Oriental mysticism.

The odds are, also, that your parents need to conform. While in minor matters they may express their independence, by and large they want to be like their neighbors so they will be liked by their neighbors. It may be hard to think of your parents being insecure (or maybe it's easy and obvious). You may think it's silly or stupid to spend so much time doing things for the purpose of courting another's favor. They don't dare step too far out of line from their fellow workers or bosses, or neighbors, for they fear their criticism. To them this is one of the realities of life: You've got to conform and compromise; otherwise you'll become an outcast. So when you express your interest in

Zen, they've got to tell you that it won't work for you here in the USA.

At this point you may well shrug it off, saying, "That's *their* hangup." But it's useful for you to realize that **they have to think this way, because it's what they learned before they had a chance to think things out, it's doubtless what their parents believed, and if they ever changed their views, or supported your having other beliefs, their guilt feelings would be enormous.** They might feel that they were desecrating the memories of *their* parents, that they might be crushed by the entire Church structure falling on them, or even more personally, they might be castigated by the Voice of God, or snuffed out by His Hand.

All of this, of course, is not intended to discourage you, or anything, from being a Zen Buddhist; it's just to give you some idea of how your parents got to think the way they do.

On the other hand—no offense intended—how'd you get to be a Zen Buddhist?

Morals And Other Human Values (A Brief Guide To Human Confusion)

Parents do and say many, many things. Some of the things they do make their children very happy, most are so everyday that they're taken for granted and generally go by unnoticed, but some of the things parents do have such a negative effect on their kids that they may cancel out all the good works they perform. It's kind of tragic that this happens, because some parents who are pretty good people end up looking like monsters to their children. How does this come about?

First of all, it isn't deliberate on the part of parents. They don't mean to be mean; indeed they fully believe that they're acting in the best interests of you guys, their beloved offspring (well, beloved most of the time). However, they get involved in an age-old dilemma, which we'd like you to hear about, because it keeps coming up over and over again.

To put it briefly, parents tell you things that begin with the stomachache-producing phrases: *you should* or *you shouldn't*, or their equivalents, such as *you ought to* or *you'd better*, and so forth. Sometimes the *should* turns into a *must*, and sometimes it's eliminated altogether and simply comes out, "Eat your cauliflower." But whether the *should* is spoken or not it's certainly there by implication, and so is the further implication that you *should* because it's *right* that you should. Moreover it's implied that it's *wrong* if you don't, and also that *you're* wrong if you don't, and ultimately that you're *bad* if you don't. So the entire sequence gets short-circuited, and when your parents say that you *should* or you *shouldn't* you react the same way as if they're saying *you're wrong* or *pure evil*—even though you know that nobody's pure anything.

There's another way of looking at this that comes out pretty much the same. When your parents say that you should do something (or not, as the case may be), you immediately get the feeling that they're trying to control you. It follows that you don't want them to control you, because you want to have control over yourself. If your parents feel that they have to control you, this means to you that they feel that you can't control yourself, that is, left to yourself, you're out of control, or uncontrolled, willful, negativistic, recalcitrant, naughty, or just plain *bad*, which is the same place we came out before. So it amounts to the same thing.

Let's say it's Saturday afternoon and you and your friend are going to a rock concert. Your father says that you should mow the lawn. He used that word *should*, which means that it's right, correct, proper, necessary, and essential to your family and, no doubt, to the whole human race for you to mow the lawn. But you say you *can't* because you have something you have to do. Your father says, "What do you mean you have something to do! What you have to do is to mow the lawn!"

"But," you say, "I have a previous engagement."

"You mean you have a date to go to the rock concert! It's more important for you to mow the lawn!"

You literally see red. Too old to cry, you find yourself flying into a rage. You hear yourself saying, "I don't have 'dates,' and there's no such thing as a 'rock concert.' I don't know what 'rock' is. 'Rock' is a large stone. Parents go to concerts," you add haughtily. Did you say all that? Yes you did. You heard yourself say it.

Your father calls your mother. "I can't talk to your child," he tells her. "Your child won't mow the lawn, tells me he doesn't have 'dates,' and says there's no such thing as a 'rock concert.' "

Your mother says, "Don't be disrespectful to your father. Remember that you have to respect him because he's the head of this family."

You hear yourself saying to your dismay, "He's a creep and you're a creep." You storm up to your room muttering, "They have to make a moral issue out of everything!"

You will be happy to learn that this entire unfortunate incident is shortly resolved. You do mow the lawn and you do take your girl to the rock concert. You will also be happy to learn that your position in this incident is correct, even though your having a temper tantrum is way outside the baseline. Your parents were making a moral issue of something that is not logically a moral issue, and this resulted in rather unproductive emotional outbursts on all sides.

The error that your parents make (and that everyone makes at one time or another) is in treating you as if you were a small child. If you're old enough to run a power mower (and old enough to drive a car and take a friend to a concert), you're old enough to be treated as having some practical judgment. It follows that you are able to

54

negotiate, to make deals, to set priorities; in short, *to behave rationally and maturely.* And you know that in your own life (away from home, that is) you're able to make decisions and to come to terms with other people. It's just much harder to do this with your parents, especially when they make you feel like a child.

While it's a mistake to treat an adolescent as though he's a child, the error is a perfectly understandable one. It's obvious when you look at someone who's eighteen or nineteen years old that he or she can't be treated as though they were six or seven. But what's the point at which a parent is going to change over from showing and telling a small child precisely what to do in each situation, to giving more general instructions to a fairly responsible adolescent and expecting him to figure out for himself how to go about it? Is it at twelve? Thirteen? Fifteen? Eighteen? We could make a bad joke of it and say, "Never," but that isn't really what parents intend.

The real answer, of course, is that you can't give any specific age, and you certainly can't say it's the same age for everything. While a parent might let a seven-year-old have absolute freedom in deciding which flavor ice cream cone he wants, that same parent might give that same son or daughter, now seventeen, absolutely *no* choice in deciding whether or not to finish high school. *So it might seem to parents that some questions are too important to be decided by young people.*

It certainly isn't too hard to accept the idea that parents feel responsibility for their children, at least until the time that their sons and daughters are more or less completely on their own. When their children are very small, parents have to take complete responsibility, and it isn't surprising that they get into a habit, which they find hard to break *even after they realize that their children are now able to handle many matters for themselves. Thus it is only natural that they slip back into the habit of telling adolescents what they should and should not do.* This is especially true when sons and daughters make life choices cwhich are different from those which their parents would have preferred them to make. It is at times like this that parents tend to turn matters of preference or simple priority into "moral issues," that is, questions of right and wrong, good and evil.

Whatever else religion and morality may be, they are—without question—forces for controlling people's behavior, and this focuses most strongly on young people. All religions have rules of behavior, the most obvious of which is the Ten Commandments, a series of statements about what *thou shalt* and what *thou shalt not.* If you break one of the Ten Commandments, or some similar rule, you tend to feel guilty.

Normally, people do not like to feel guilty, and so they get angry at other people who make them feel that way. Kids are angry at parents who arouse feelings of guilt, although they are often afraid to express their anger, and this may produce other painful feelings, such as headaches or stomachaches.

In the same way that kids get angry at their parents for what seems to be excessive control, people get angry at religions. When people of any age feel that the religious climate in which they have been raised is overly controlling, that is, too full of *shoulds* and *should nots,* they get angry at it, and want to change it. This is one of the reasons for so-called "reform" movements in religion. An "orthodox" or "strict" interpretation of the laws of God or of the Universe makes a group of people too uncomfortable, and they break away, forming a sect of their own, interpreting natural law in a way they find more acceptable. (Sometimes they end up with an even more strict interpretation, but that's another story; things often go back and forth.) Sometimes some people decide that all religions are no good and that there should be no morality or no laws (these are the outlaws, criminals), but generally people end up with some kind of rules.

The world's great religions tend to teach that there is a God, some kind of controlling Force in the Universe, and that we should live according to His Law. They also teach that we should, in some sense, love our neighbors and deal fairly with them. We are all brought up to believe this in some form. However, we are also brought up to believe that God helps those who help themselves, that each of us should look out for Number One (that's you), and that we should do unto our neighbor as he would do unto us—but that we should do it first. We all learn to conform to the ways of society with respect to getting a good education, but we also see that a surprising number of improperly educated people establish themselves as self-proclaimed experts, and appear to get away with it! We learn that one of the biggest and most successful businesses in this country is organized crime, and we learn that some of the wealthiest people in the world never did any productive labor and don't pay any taxes. We also learn that sex is a beautiful and meaningful experience, but that very many well-known people seem to be very casual about with whom they go to bed and under what circumstances.

The word "morals" is derived from the Latin word "mores," which meant something like "customs" or "manners." This may be a useful way to think about things; *it may be more comfortable to understand moral principles as simply the way the natives around here do things* (rather than as something you'll be struck dead for if you don't follow it precisely).

In most families the idea of "customs" or "style" or "manners" is probably a more accurate way of describing the way things are done than it would be to say that there's a strict religious code. Family custom or family style is passed on from parents to children, so what your parents believe is right probably reflects more what *their* parents believed than what was taught to them by a minister, priest, rabbi, shaman, or guru.

Of course this doesn't mean that you may respond to your family's not eating meat on Fridays by saying that this is strictly a local custom not observed by all of the local natives, and therefore you don't have to conform (as you pull the hamburger out of your pocketbook). What parents believe in has to be respected, just as you expect them to respect you when you refuse to eat any meat at all, blandly advising all within earshot that you have just joined the Reform Vegetarian Church.

What people should and shouldn't do can become a vicious game unless everyone realizes that the most important aspect of morality or custom is that it has to work, to perform some useful function other than merely to control one another by creating guilt feelings. This ideal may only be approached by mutual respect and, perhaps needless to say, respect has to be earned. Parents will continue to tell their offspring what to do until said offspring are able to demonstrate good judgment, personal responsibility, and a reasonable amount of achievement in the outside world. Of course some parents will go right on telling adolescents what to do regardless of their age, good sense, and personal accomplishments, but—as we may have said before—who promised that everything in this life is fair?

7

The Truth About SEX (And Other Assorted Myths)

When it comes to sex there's good news and bad news. The good news is that there's really not much that any of us has to understand about it. And that same piece of information is also the bad news.

It is a fact that nearly every one of us living on this earth was conceived as a direct result of a male and female having sexual intercourse (the exceptions being a relatively few pregnancies which are achieved by artificial insemination). This undeniable truth carries on its back a significant corollary: all kinds of people are capable of having sexual relations: tall, short, fat, thin, pretty, ugly, smart, stupid, with-it, out-of-it, and so on. Most important, you hardly have to know what you're doing in order to perform the sex act. Indeed, it is ridiculously easy to conceive a baby. And it's somewhat startling, or even staggering, to realize that some 15 or 20 years ago a man and woman who might have hardly known each other, and who didn't necessarily like each other, and who might have been drunk, felt sexually turned on because they were alone together, or happy, or unhappy, or angry at two other people, and put their sex organs together and conceived a child who might have beaten you out for the swimming team, or gotten the guy or girl you wanted, or bumped into your car, or perhaps even helped you by pulling your car out of a ditch or loaning you ten dollars, or might have grown up to become anyone...even you!

So, as we said, it's both good news and bad news, or maybe neither good nor bad, but just—how it is.

When your parents ask you if you know "the facts of life," they want to know if you realize how easy it is to cause a pregnancy, that is, if you're not careful, if you don't take precautions, if you do what comes naturally, if you let nature take its course, if you follow your normal impulses, if you give in to your sex drive. In other words if you behave perfectly *normally*, someone is going to get pregnant.* But "the facts of life" have to do with more than pregnancy. Even today, in our supposedly sexually enlightened era, most people are not capable of a truly natural, conflict-free expression of their sexuality. When a sexual joke or allusion is made, we giggle. Gossip about the sexual activities of a neighbor, business colleague or public figure holds much interest for us all. While, in general, we tend to condemn the subjects of such gossip, the

---

*Of course you realize that we're all biologically programmed that way, presumably to insure the survival of the human race. However, there may be a difference between what is good for the human race and what is good for you: at this particular time in your life it may not be convenient for you to have a baby because you probably have a number of things that you want to do and having a baby would probably tie you down and prevent you from doing them. Even though it's reasonably easy to get an abortion, there are some possible unpleasantnesses of a physical, emotional or social nature that could follow, and it's generally better not to have to go that way. There are also a variety of approaches to contraception that you probably know about, and if you're grown up enough to have sexual intercourse you're also grown up enough to learn about and use contraception. Your parents, however, may tell you that there's only one really sure means of contraception, and that's abstinence: not having any sexual intercourse at all.

fact that this gossip is so newsworthy speaks to a more secret side of ourselves that is curious. Most of us, however mature or sexual, never lose that child-like curiosity about sex. Some element of the mysterious, the unfathomable remains within us, no matter how experienced we may be. We continue to have, in private, our questions of what we are missing, of what experiences might be like with someone else, of how ridiculous or wrong it is for us to even think such thoughts, or have such fantasies. Yet we continue with thoughts and fantasies, for our attitudes towards sexuality are part prurient, part puritanical. We swing from desire to suppression of desire, and back and forth. Our attitudes are anything but natural; that is, they are not free from tension or conflict. This conflict within your parents is something they will not share with you, something you are likely not to sense. But it is there, behind their telling you of "the facts of life."

It's hard to prove this one way or another, but it's probably true that, regardless of what they say, most parents wish that their adolescent sons and daughters (especially daughters) would just plain stay away from sex. There is a very good reason for this: if sex, because of pregnancy, or whatever follows, interferes with the social, educational, or economic development of their adolescent children, the responsibility (social, economic, moral) falls back on the parents, and they simply don't want it. And there is a not very good reason for this also: Adults like to be sentimental about the young and like to see the young as being "innocent," that is, free from sin and corruption (= sex). Adults tend to forget that they were sexually active (in feeling, thought and desire) from a very young age themselves and that sexual fantasies, if not actual experiences, preoccupied much of their time during their adolescences. In "protecting" you from your sexuality they attempt to sustain the illusion that you are "pure"—"uncorrupted" and "innocent."

So the parent ends up essentially saying, "Sex is OK for us, but it isn't OK for you." What that statement comes down to is, "Sex is OK for us *because we're prepared to deal with the consequences.*"

On the other hand, however, there's all that pressure to think and feel sexual, to look sexual and act sexual and maybe, get *into* the sex act! There are all those exciting feelings inside you, and all those beautiful bodies belonging to members of the opposite sex, and everyone talking about it, and everything in books and magazines and newspapers, and on radio, and on TV and in the movies and on the stage (and not just the X-rated stuff, either), all of which seems to be aimed at *you!* Sometimes it seems as though the whole world is trying to turn you on!

Sometimes (about 99% of the time) you feel that there may be something wrong with you because you seem to be thinking about sex all the time. You're in school, sitting in class, and the teacher is talking about Oliver Cromwell and the Roundheads, about the Puritans, yet, and suddenly, without even asking your permission, sexual thoughts enter your head! Your head? They enter *all* of you. You are permeated with sexual feeling and desire. Or you may be sitting in church, with the minister intoning ennobling ideas, when you see a head three pews in front of you, and you identify the head as belonging to someone your own age, someone of the opposite sex. It is only the back of a head, but you know that on the front of that head are eyes and a nose and a mouth, and that below that head is a body. And the next thing you know you have all kinds of exciting thoughts about that body, and you feel embarrassed because you are in church and should be thinking about *higher* things. What a problem! But the worst part (or the best, depending on how you look at it) is in your dreams, where the sex act is miraculously consummated with evidence that is visible the next morning, though your partner seems to have vanished during the night.

So you feel that, yes, you must be some kind of sexual monster, suffering from satyriasis or nymphomania: those horrible words that don't have any disease associated with them. Mostly you think you're so weird that you don't even check things out with your peer group, with kids your own age. But if you did, you'd find that they're mostly just like you, only some of them have it worse!

Well, you reason, pretty soon I'll grow up and get over all this. Obviously, older people are not as interested in sex as young people. Older people are busy with lots of other things. They're busy building shopping centers and starting depressions and wars and outlawing pot, porno (which is their thing, not yours), and fun in general. They can be with a member of the opposite sex and not get nervous or perhaps even terrified for fear of getting overwhelmed by sexual desire and doing something immoral or illegal right in broad daylight and in front of other people. Right?

Wrong! As well as we can figure out, most people spend a good bit of their entire lives thinking sexual thoughts. Indeed, people can only accomplish most things because they have more or less "sexualized" them: because they have invested into these objects, goals, or activities some of the emotional charge that's ordinarily reserved for sex, or because they lead up to sex or because they result in or heighten sexual desire or satisfaction. In other words, people really have to get turned on by something in order to do a good job. Otherwise what they do is routine, or rote, or boring, or they simply hate it. Sometimes, of course, people can't do something because it's sexualized for them, but those people are usually frightened by their own sexuality.

Now you may feel that this way of thinking is somewhat theoretical and is only one way of looking at things, but, if you consider yourself, you can immediately think of how you do things to impress members of the other sex, or in order to please them, or to make money to spend on dates, or on clothes or a car which will be attractive in the eyes of the one who is attractive in your eyes. Don't you believe that older people are the same and behave the same way?

We assume that your father and mother are responsible people and will avoid doing things that threaten the ongoing security of your family life. That is, we assume that they are mature. It is almost an old joke that kids can't believe that their parents have sexual relations with each other, but you know that they do, and you may even have seen or heard them making love. You also have to realize that they find other people sexually attractive, and not only TV and movie stars, but other people they know socially and at work. And they certainly have sexual thoughts about these other people, and in a considerable number of cases may have done sexual things with them. But that is their business, and we assume that they are able to handle these matters without wrecking their lives.

Which brings us back again to the basic idea that almost everyone is interested in sex, and this even includes very old people like your grandparents and perhaps great-grandparents, if they're not too incapacitated. Older people are more socially skillful, and may not be quite as obvious about their sexual interests as a nine, fourteen, or nineteen-year-old. Therefore you may be led into mistaking their cool for disinterest. No, *what really distinguishes older from younger people is their improved ability to hold back, to wait for a better time, to make more careful choices, to take responsibility for the consequences of their behavior.*

Your parents may not always be right, or moral, or wise in what they do sexually, as in all other things, but again, as in all other things, they believe that they are trying to teach you to handle sex better, perhaps better than they do or did.

On the other hand, your parents may not be as mature and responsible about sex as we have assumed. And they may not be as honest with you as we would all like, because they are not being honest with themselves. In that case, **you will have to do a lot more thinking, and living, and thinking, and living, and a lot of talking with other people who are at least as wise and experienced as you, and who may be able to see your situation more objectively than you can.**

It is tremendously important that you learn to appreciate sex in a positive, healthy, and rational way, because, whether your parents handle it well or not, it can be the most wonderful and important part of life that any of us experiences.

Part III

THE SECRET WORLD
OF ADULTS
(THEY CALL IT "REALITY")

Parents sometimes tell you that "you're too young to understand." But when they tell you nothing, or give you mixed or contradictory messages, or when they tell you outright lies, what is there to understand? What is the mysterious adult world that permits its members to be unfaithful to each other or to walk out on spouse or job or become an alcoholic or gambler or deadbeat?

8

The Nature Of Human Communication

"Communication" has become a very popular word in recent years. Everyone uses it to describe what they do achieve and what other people don't. Most of the time each of us knows (or thinks he knows) what he wants to say and each feels he knows how to say it. So we are surprised when we are misunderstood.

Of course, "communication" is a very popular word with your parents. That's what they say they're always trying to get into with you and what, for some unexplainable reason, you ingrates—with your hearts of stone—refuse to get into with them. If only you would confide in them (after all, who cares for you more than they); if only you would listen to their wise counsel (after all, they have only your best interests at heart); if only you would tell them what you're about and where you're going (after all, they worry about you so much); if only you would *communicate* with them, then there wouldn't be one-tenth the hassles and conflicts there are in the family!

Sounds familiar, doesn't it? Gets you mad enough at times that you tell yourself that even under pain of extreme torture, you won't divulge one word, one thought, one opinion—even if your life depends on it!

All of us have problems communicating, and understanding the communications of others. Your parents are no exception. And neither are you. Then what are the special problems parents have in talking with you?

For openers, there are the communicational problems associated with being the authority. Conversation tends to be one-way: "Wash the dishes." "Clean up your room." "Don't lean on your elbows at dinner." "Do your homework." They are the captains. And you are the foot-soldiers. They give the orders. You follow them.

Often the orders are not so blatant: "You could do me a big favor by washing the dishes." "I think you would feel much better if you cleaned up your room." "You know, it's bad manners to lean on your elbows at the dinner table." "Don't you think it's time to do your homework?" But they are orders, nonetheless. The message is quite clear even when it is worded in a more reasonable, non-authoritarian manner. "Do as I say...Don't give me any back talk." Well, why don't you "do it"? What stops you from doing what you know you have to do, what you may even think is reasonable to do, and what you even may want to do? Why do you freeze, procrastinate and consequently invite your parents to bark their orders again? Why is it that when you're sitting at breakfast and your mother gently reminds you to be sure to feed the dog before you go off to school, you stare out the window and don't move. She reminds you again, a little less gently, but you still don't move. You love the dog and don't want to do anything to harm him, but you resist feeding him. Inside, you feel a little tension and some irritability. "Get off of my back," you think. "I know I've got to feed the dog." You don't like to be told the obvious and treated as though you haven't the mental capacity to remember a simple chore from day to day. You see out of the corner of your eye that your mother is bristling now. And you sense that in a short time she will pounce again with, "You didn't feed the dog yesterday. I had to feed him. We might as well get rid of him for all you care about him."

She got you good this time. You didn't feed him yesterday, not because you don't care about him, but because of your resistance to your mother's authoritarianism. And now she's got you on two counts: *irresponsibility* and *guilt*. It would be worth a try to say that your not feeding the dog had nothing to do with caring for the dog, and everything to do with not liking to be ordered around. But more likely than not, your mother wouldn't be in the right emotional state to tolerate it at that moment and might see it as a feeble rationalization on your part.

There's something very curious here. In our travels through life thus far, we've encountered very few people who like to receive orders, but a lot of people (not excluding ourselves) who like to give orders. Could it be that this is one instance where humankind actually practices the golden rule that says it is better to give than to receive?

A second problem of communication commonly seen in parents' transactions with their kids is that of giving *mixed messages*. Varying from mild sarcasm ("Gosh, Paul. You're really agile"—Paul just having dropped and smashed a glass) to outright "double-binds,"* the mixed message allows the sender to control the receiver by being ambiguous and confusing.

Have you ever had the experience of approaching your father about what to do on a Saturday? Let's say he's cleaning out the garage, trying to put in order several years

---

*A "double-bind" communication is a highly complex and ambiguous interpersonal message wherein the sender controls the receiver with paradox and confusion. A classic example would be, "Disobey me." If you obey the message, you paradoxically must disobey. If you disobey the message and seek to obey, you carry out the spirit of the message by disobeying it. Either way you're caught. No way out. A "Catch-22" is a variant on the double-bind.

of disarray and mess. You think that maybe he wants you to help him, but you're not particularly hot about the idea. Maybe you want to toss the ball around with a friend or just go uptown and hang around. But you think you ought to ask him first. "Dad, do you need any help or can I go uptown?" And he answers wisely and compassionately, "Of course, I can use any help I can get. But you can make your own decision as to what you want to do." Phooey. He doesn't give you the choice. He lets you know exactly what he wants and makes you squirm at the same time. If, by mistake, you should heed your wishes rather than your duty, you'll pay for it sooner or later.

There are many such scenes where the message is unclear on a verbal level, but very clear on a gut level, where presumably you have free choice...as long as you make the *right* decision.

A different type of mixed message falls under the rubric of "The grass isn't always greener, or is it?" Mom is concerned about your friends. She thinks that they're really not good enough for you and they lead you astray, causing you to slough your schoolwork and making you insolent at home. "Don't you think it's time," she asks, "for you to stop following that crowd and learn to think for yourself? These friends of yours are no good and they're having a bad influence on you. You ought to trust yourself more and learn to take independent action ....Why don't you spend more time with Johnny Jones? He knows how to think for himself." Hey. Wait a minute. She just got through saying you shouldn't follow the crowd around. And now she's telling you to switch to a different crowd. What's she really saying? What's the real message? It's hard to say. It seems that maybe she doesn't want you to think for yourself. It was thinking for yourself that got you with the crowd you're with, after all.

And you think it's not so much their "bad influence" on you, but your influence on them that keeps the crowd going. But she doesn't think you have a mind of your own. Better you should be led around by someone who's "nicer" and more earnest. Nuts! When you confront her with your view of the situation she says that that's not it at all, that you're twisting her words, that she thinks you have a mind of your own if only you'd use it, that etc., etc., etc. And so it goes. Let me out of here!

Or how about the one when the dreaded aunt is coming to visit. There's no question that she doesn't like you, never did, and always has a fixed, ingratiating smile plastered on her face. Two years ago, at Christmas, she sent you a shirt that was so God-awful ugly and unwearable that the whole family howled with laughter over it. Yet you still had to write her a thank-you note telling her how "the colors are really neat and go with my purple skirt," which you don't have. Now, with Auntie coming, Mom reminds you how much "Auntie really loves you and is looking forward to hearing all about what you have been doing." Do you listen to your mother who is trying to modify and shape your perception of your aunt or do you listen to yourself? Do you act as if you cared for her, thus placating your mother, while being dishonest to yourself? Or do you act on what you believe, thus incurring your mother's displeasure?

A well known actor tells the story of how his father, also an actor, tried to dissuade him from going on the stage. "It's a rough way to make a living...Dog-eat-dog competition. Get into something more stable, a profession like medicine...But don't slouch...Look how you drag yourself when you come into a room. Stand up straight...And don't mumble your words. Project your voice...Learn to project." Some mixed message. The son

72

said there was never any real question in his mind that he would become an actor. He heard his father's real message ("meta message" is what communications specialists call it), the message that had the most emotional force, and that's what he acted on.

Nearly all families adhere to the ethical norms within the community. Thus, it is important to be honest and never lie. It is wrong to cheat. One must love thy neighbor as thyself and have high regard and respect for all, whatever their race or social class. Yet how often have you caught your parents in a deliberate lie? Odds are that you've caught them many times. "Well," they say, if you point it out, "there are special circumstances where one has to tell a small lie for the good of all concerned, perhaps to prevent a greater lie." Rubbish. If they can justify their lies, why not your lies? What makes you so different?

Same thing with cheating and stealing. You've got to be a Boy Scout or Girl Scout and never ever stray from the path of righteousness. But they, being adults, can bend the rules. Maybe a little cheating of Uncle Sam on the income tax. Maybe going too fast in the car. Maybe pulling a fast one in a business deal or bringing home some goods from the plant. Is it possible that, once initiated into the rites of adulthood, one has special powers that allow one to break the rules that you are supposed to live by? After all, Mr. Nixon's plumbers performed those "dirty tricks" only because of their patriotic desire to preserve democracy for our country. Right? You got it.

The same with racial, religious and social equality. Unless you're from an exceptional family, you've been getting mixed messages right along about "loving thy neighbor." You're probably encouraged to be comfortable with a wide variety of people from the melting pot. But think twice before you get romantic with someone who's not of your race, religion or social class. We dare say that at the least, you'll strain and compromise your parents' ideals.

Under *mixed messages* the communication of sexual subjects really falls into a class all its own and needs special treatment. Do you remember the time when your dad first spoke to you about SEX (maybe because he found you writing or saying an obscenity or drawing a picture of a naked woman), how he said sex was natural and beautiful, a wonderful part of life, etc., but he couldn't look at you. He looked at the wall. He looked at his fingernails. He glanced at you and looked away. He seemed decidedly uncomfortable and unnatural as he was telling you how natural sex was. Most parents, however liberal and relaxed they may be about their own sexuality, have a hard time talking about sex with their kids. In part it's because of the child in them, the child that still thinks sex is dirty.* In part it's because the sentimental and naive adult in them thinks that you, the child, are still pure, conveniently forgetting that they, when kids, thought a heck of a lot about sex long before they ever reached puberty. In part it's because they feel they have to protect you. But why do they have to protect you if it's so natural and beautiful? The sum of all the parts is that your parents' attitudes don't make much sense and are really illogical.

"Anytime, Mary, you have any questions, please come to me and I'll do my best to answer them," says Mother, worriedly. "I think, John, it might be helpful if you read a book. It might do you good to learn a little human anatomy. Maybe they'll discuss this in your health class," says Dad, trying to take control of the situation with double-talk and evasion.

---

*Woody Allen was once asked if he thought sex was dirty. He replied, "If it's done right."

But of course these forays into explaining the "birds and the bees" are only the beginning steps of a not very well-choreographed ballet about sex that your parents and you will dance during your adolescence. Naturally you're clumsy. You don't know what it's safe to talk about, what questions it's OK to ask. And you're frightened and excited at the same time. Since there's a part of you that feels there's something wrong with your interest and preoccupation with sex, when you want to read *Fear of Flying* but you don't want your mom to know about it. You hide it in a "safe" place, under your mattress, and lo and behold, she discovers it. "Paul," she says, "It's OK to read *Fear of Flying*. But why are you hiding it under your bed?" Is it OK? Can you know, for certain, that Mom really isn't upset by what you're reading? Is she saying for real that it's all right for you to read that book? Or is she giving you a double message with the hidden part being that you shouldn't waste your time on that dirty stuff and should get down to your math?

Now you may not know, because being found out certainly raises your anxiety level. Or you may not know because your parents themselves are clumsy when it comes to talking about sex in a plain and straight manner—especially with their kids. Most people in our culture—no matter how enlightened or progressive or liberal—tend to have conflicts, hangups, around sexual topics and emotions. And while your parents are sexually experienced (though it may seem to you that they're not) they continue to have conflicts within themselves that they may project onto you. When one person projects an inner conflict on another, he usually tends to go to extremes, either the extreme of suppression or the extreme of permissiveness.

Two examples may underscore this point. At night you may wish to have your bedroom door closed and, possibly, be under the covers without pajamas on. All the better to have a sensual, auto-erotic experience. Your dad comes in the room, senses you are naked under the covers and tells you to 1) put your pajamas back on because it's unhealthy to be naked and you'll catch a cold; and 2) keep the door open (so that you'll be in a draft). Although he hasn't said a word about sex or masturbation, you quickly get the message that that's what he's really concerned about. He has projected onto you certain concerns and internal conflicts of his and tried to suppress you with indirect and bogus reasonings.

What is the message Mother gives her daughter Suzy in the following short story? Suzy is to start high school shortly. She's transferring from a Catholic girls' school to a non-sectarian public high school. Mom advises Suzy thus; "Remember, you're transferring from a small, protective environment and going to a large school. The way to survive is to study very hard. I know that's difficult. When I first went to public school after having been in parochial school all those years, I looked around and there were cute guys everywhere. I'd never seen so many cute guys. I remember especially one who was better looking than all the others. I couldn't keep my eyes off him and concentrate on study. I know the same thing will happen to you. But remember, the most important thing is to study very hard." How do you think Suzy's liable to hear her mother's advice? Will she have the fortitude not to be distracted from her studies by "cute guys" or will she listen to the "meta message," which is about exciting and titillating forbidden fruit, and watch the guys? Wearing the mask of a counselor, mother is subtly directing Suzy to begin her courtship of men. If Suzy gets too boy-crazy, Mother can throw up her hands and remonstrate against her for not heeding her admonition against flirting.

We hope *you've* gotten the message that **parents don't always mean what they say and say what they mean. Sometimes a parent may be aware of the double messages projected, other times not.** The father who goes into the bedroom does have a sense of what his child is doing and is trying to stop him from doing it without actually talking about it. In the case of Suzy, her mother was probably not attuned to how much she was programming her daughter's budding interest in boys. But it can add up to a pretty confusing picture for you. **You've got to listen very carefully and try to hear what the real message is.**

More Talk About Talk (How Can I Communicate When You're Making So Much Noise?)

You've gone and done it this time. No question about it. It was bad enough when your dad came home and greeted you with an ingratiating "Hi, Mary! how's your day been?" You could see he was tense and trying to cover it up. His tenseness irritated you so you didn't answer and made matters worse. And he said, "What's wrong with you?"

And he asked you again and you said, "Nothing." That got him more tense but he still was trying to cover it up. Then Billy came in to say that dinner was ready. Billy and Dad horsed around until Mom shouted from the kitchen that the food was getting cold. You all went to the kitchen.

Dad said to you, "If there's something wrong, I'd wish you'd tell me what it is," and you said, "Nothing. I told you there was nothing wrong."

"What's bothering her?" Dad asked Mom.

"I don't know. I never know," said Mom. "Let's try not

to fight tonight. Let's see if we can get through just one meal without anyone fighting or getting angry. For once let's see if we can be a family and not a bunch of snarling barbarians."

Well, you sit down to dinner and it's very tense. Dad is extra polite, the kind of polite he always is when he's a seething cauldron on the inside. And Mom looks frazzled. You're uptight, irritated, and don't feel at all hungry. You play with your food. Mom comments on how hard she worked to prepare the meal and Dad gives her a lavish compliment on how tasteful it is.

Then you go and do it, really do it big and irreversibly. "I don't like the asparagus and I'm not very hungry." Well that screws things royally. Dad blows up, waves his fork at you and tells you to "damn well eat your asparagus."

Mom says, "For once could we not scream at one another and upset dinner?" She begins to cry, puts down her fork and leaves the table. "Now I'm not hungry either."

Dad's cauldron boils over. "I've had it. Had a very rough day at the office and I come home to this. What do I need this for? I'm not hungry either." And so he leaves and goes to the den.

You knew you should have kept your mouth shut and choked on the asparagus. You could have muddled through the meal even though you felt like puking. But you opened your mouth and blew it, upset the whole family, wrecked the dinner and sent everyone running for cover.

A dramatic scene? Perhaps. Hopefully not in your household. But unfortunately, not an uncommon scene in many households and with many families. Why is it that arguments tend to cluster around mealtime and seem to center on the actions of the children? There are many

complex reasons concerning family interaction, of which
we will touch on only a few. In the above drama Mary is
seen as the villain in her parents' eyes. She does not answer her father when he attempts to initiate conversation.
When he responds with irritation, she snarls back at him.
Surely a daughter could greet her father with a warm welcome as he comes home from work. But she doesn't.
They are tense as they go to the dinner table. Mom has
labored to provide a good meal and also wants acknow-
ledgment for her work. While Dad compliments her the
two children remain silent. Then Mary says something,
obviously critical and provocative, that causes the explo-
sion and the destruction of dinner.

But it is not as simple as that. For the four have each
come from a hard day's activity (work, school, household
chores) and each enters with a certain amount of tension
and fatigue. Mary may be uptight, but so is Dad. He is
trying to pretend that he is in a good mood when he obviously isn't. He could have ignored Mary's silent provo-
cation, or if he had picked up on it in a more supportive
way, such as "Heck, maybe you've had as rough a day as
I've had. Boy, I'm beat and on edge," chances are Mary
might have been better able to respond. She could have
acknowledged she had a tough day, or not, or she could
have inquired about her father's day. In some way she
and Dad might have been able to get a conversation going, or at least they might have had some better sense of
how each was feeling. But by this not happening, it
helped set the stage for what followed.

Mother also helped. Her wish that the family could have a
calm and peaceful meal together was expressed as a consequence of many past unpleasant meals and also in response
to her picking up the ambient tension. But in making her
wish not to have tension, she inadvertently helped to esca-
late the tension. She could have moved in a more direct and

supportive way—such as by pointing out the tension and bringing the family together to discuss it—and perhaps might have dissipated it somewhat. But in consequence of this not happening, the final scene took place.

And Mary got the blame for it. Mary goes off feeling resentful, angry, muttering that her parents are both crazy and that she can't wait until she can get out of the house for good. But part of her feels guilty. She is upset that she didn't greet her father, that she was provocative to him and that she blew it at the table. So while she may outwardly deny it, she inwardly carries the burden for this fracas.

Yet the truth is that her parents are as much, if not more, responsible for what happened. For better or for worse, the parents are the leaders for the family and set the tone for what happens within the group. In this incident, they abdicated their responsibilities for leadership by denying their own tensions, tensions which were independent of and unrelated to Mary's tensions, and they "scapegoated" Mary, that is, dumped the burdens for what happened excessively on her. The argument thus serves for parents as a mechanism whereby they can discharge their own worries and concerns on another person, their child.

The onus for communicating is on Mary. Her "Nothing" sets off her father and starts the family argument. Overlooked by the whole family is that her father also said "Nothing," by not talking about his tensions, his problems of the day. Indeed his failure to communicate and his clumsy and obvious attempt to cover-up his true emotions by being over-solicitous and ingratiating was the true beginning of the family drama.

Thus sometimes as much is communicated by what is *not* said as by what *is* said. Silence can be as perilous (or even more so) as sound, the quiet from what is held back is perhaps even more damaging than the harshness of what is thrown out. When angered or discontented, we all tend to one of two common reactions: either lashing out, seeking to hurt or wound, or retreating into ourselves, sulking and petulant in our silence. We adults, parents, are unfortunate but highly effective role-models for you, our children. We teach you our ways, then criticize you when you follow them. We have our cake and eat it too.

While not all families have fights, few have a true calmness and orderly working together, because *interpersonal conflict is inevitable whenever people live or work in close proximity to one another.* Petty jealousies, hurts and slights—these are the stuff of life. They cannot be avoided, will not go away if we close our eyes or deafen our ears, if we try to turn our backs on them. Yet some families, again led by the parents, attempt to do just this. They imagine that if they do not speak ill, there is no ill. If they do not bicker, there is nothing to bicker about, if they do not have rancor, then they have harmony.

James comes from such a family. There is a quiet in his house that is eerie. His brother and sister have gone off to college and he is alone with his parents. Not that it was much better when they were there, except the silence is louder now that they are gone. He and his parents struggle to have kind things to say to each other. They certainly don't want to bring up any unpleasantness. So at the dinner table, for instance, they listen mostly to the sounds of their forks against their plates. After meals they scatter, Dad to the TV, James to his stereo, and Mom to her dishes.

Judy's parents on the other hand are not quiet. They are brimming with a sunshine that suffuses to every corner of every room. They rise from bed each morning without complaint and greet each day as a challenge. They do not admit defeat or despair. Nothing is impossible as long as one is willing to work and play hard. And they tend to talk in the first person plural: "We're going to have a nice day today." "How are we feeling today?" They steer all conversation deftly around potentially troublesome issues and, in their positiveness, cover up their fear of conflict. At times Judy is out of sorts and can't play the game so well, has difficulty steering away from her own discontent. At such times, Mom or Dad will urge her on to be more forceful and positive, to put aside her "petty worries," which "we all have." But we can't let those worries get us down, can we? When Judy can't or won't heed her parents' directive to put her "petty worries" away, to "forget them," she's in for a double dose of their positive thinking. Small wonder she gets confused. She comes to think that her irksome emotions have no validity.

There's no way around conflict. We complain about it, wish that it weren't there, try to cover it over, forget that it's there, but, like the weather, it stays around.

There's another rule in families, made up by parents, copied by their kids, and used increasingly successfully by them as they grow older, culminating in their becoming parents and thus able to use it with their own kids. And that is the rule of *secrets:* We are not supposed to have secrets. We are supposed to confide in our parents our innermost concerns, worries, preoccupations, obsessions, fantasies, wishes, thoughts. But we note sometime around our eighth or ninth year that our parents are not doing the same to us. Increasingly we feel like chumps for being foolish enough to be open, only to have it used against us and for not having that openness reciprocated. Did you ever ask your father how much money he makes? Chances are he told you: 1) "It's not your concern" (none of your business); 2) "Oh, enough to keep us going if we conserve" (not as much as you might hope for so you'd better watch what you spend); 3) "Enough to make ends meet" (barely getting by), or some such evasive answer. You hear Mom and him grumbling all the time about inflation, about washing machines breaking down, the price of clothes, food, fuel, everything, and you hear them telling you not to shuffle when you walk because you're wearing out your sneakers, but you probably don't have a ballpark figure for what income they have.

Or maybe you hear them arguing down in the kitchen when you're in bed at night. It sounds pretty bad. They're really angry with one another. Occasionally you can pick out a few words, or a sentence or two, enough to make you scared, but not enough to let you know what's going on between them. The next morning you ask them at breakfast what the fight was about and they say: 1) "What fight?"; 2) "Oh, Dad and I were having a minor disagreement"; 3) "We were talking about you kids"; 4) "It's none of your business." So there you are again. Stalemated. Stopped in your tracks.

You begin to adopt their ways. You learn that there are things you'd best keep to yourself, especially those things you know will make them angry (like you took your birthday money and bought a new skateboard when they never really approved of the first one), and those things which make them angry but are in the realm of "forbidden fruits" (like sex).

And, of course, they come down on you for withholding from them.

   —"How can we help you if we don't know what's going on?"

   —"This report card is a disgrace. If only you had let us know you were having trouble before."

   —"Why do you always look so frightened when I come into your room?"

—"We feel you're becoming estranged from us. Why aren't you like you used to be?"

They talk with their friends about mutual difficulties with their kids, how they don't know what's going on, how you've become strangers, sullen, withdrawn. They read magazine articles on "Understanding Your Teenagers," "The Problems of Disaffected Youth in Society Today," "Seven Danger Signals to Watch Out For When Your Child May Be Troubled." They buy books telling them how to be more effective parents, how to communicate with you better (that means "how to get you to talk more with them"), how to understand the special, unique problems youth faces today in growing up in a troubled world. They go to PTA meetings where they talk about how the school is failing you (and them) by not providing a trusting and open environment wherein communication can take place, and where they talk about "bad influences" (other kids) warping and disturbing their own loved ones.

In other words, they, being *concerned* parents, feel they do everything in their power to improve communication with you. And yet you continue not to communicate with them. But the truth is that they don't level with you. They hide from you their money troubles, their conflicts, their despairs and futility (except when you seem to be the cause of it), their infidelities, their drinking ("There's nothing wrong with me having this drink; it helps me relax after I've had a hard day"), their thoughts about wanting to run away from it all.

You may not know what is in your parents' minds, but you know there's something there that you're not hearing. And that's what you learn to do: not communicate— just as they don't—instead of *listening* for the hidden messages when they do communicate.

10
Program Notes On The Behavior Of Married People

We are all more alike than we are different. Each of us likes to think of himself as unique, as someone special, as someone apart and distinct from others. Each of us keeps a treasure-house of secrets, of wishes and dreams, hidden within. While we may dress alike and act alike and even seem to be alike, we hold to the notion that, deep down, there was no one ever before quite like us and never will be again. But the truth is, sad to say, that we are all more alike than unalike. What we value as special and unique about us is, much more likely than not, equally valued by our friends, neighbors and enemies and those we never even thought of, as what is unique about them. While each of us has individual fingerprints that sets him apart from others, we all have individual fingerprints, the differences among them being subtle and miniscule, requiring an expert to distinguish.

So it is with our relationships. Much as we fight against it, bristle at the mention of it, and do our damnedest to avoid it, we are a statistic in what we do and how we relate to others. And marriage, that most sacred of relationships, is likewise a profane statistic.

When your parents first fell in love, they had a dream. Their love would burn forever and would not be dampened or die down with the passage of time. Unlike their own parents, and other parents of their own generation, they would continually rekindle their fiery love, keep its flame ever-bright, its heat ever-intense. They were naive enough to believe, as we are all naive enough to believe, that they could defy the statistics, the realities of marriage, and go against the laws of matrimonial gravity which have stated very clearly, for millennia, that it's mostly downhill once the honeymoon is over.

But the odds are overwhelming against their defying those laws of gravity. In a matter of months, occasionally up to a year or two, the ardor diminishes and the romantic attachment subsides, pales before the mundane routine of daily living, all the irritating trivia and petty irrelevancies that make up life. We lack the endurance and the will and strength to carry out our sentiments and aspirations from day to day. Flaubert, the French literary genius, talking about love in *Madame Bovary*, put it thus: "...No one can ever express the exact measure of his needs, his conceptions or his sorrows, and human speech is like a cracked pot on which we beat out rhythms for bears to dance to when we are striving to make music that will wring tears from the stars." We are all faced with the disparity between what we would like to be and what we actually are. And we are stuck with the limitations of our real selves.

Slowly, inexorably, the routine takes over in married life as it does in all aspects of life. Your parents, after the high pitch of romance and novelty had waned, settled into the rut of daily living and had to confront dirty socks left on the bedroom floor; washing of clothes, dishes, floors, windows, cars, selves; what to do—if anything—on Saturday night; TV football weekends vs. TV melodramas; not talking; talking about scratches on the coffee table; talking about having the in-laws in for Sunday dinner; talking about how things are going or not going at work and with the neighbors. And so it goes. Not very lofty nor imbued with high drama. Very domestic, seemingly random and chaotic.

Yet this behavior, in addition to being all too typical and predictable, is highly patterned, purposeful and even productive. We can easily identify four modes of behavior that couples act out concerning each other in a cyclical, repetitive and structured way. They are 1) those behaviors concerning survival and maintenance matters; 2) those behaviors, with themselves and especially with others, related by a highly choreographed and ritualized social dance; 3) those behaviors related to attachment—expressions of love and affection; 4) those behaviors related to distancing—fighting, withdrawing.

1) *Survival* issues are first and foremost on almost everyone's list. Keeping bread on the table and in the pocket, paying the rent and mortgage, getting, buying, acquiring, replacing, repairing, fixing, struggling to keep out of hock, trying to put a little aside for a vacation or for a rainy day—these are a few of the money concerns that seem to consume couples and drown out preoccupations with philosophy and romance. While money concerns are paramount, they are not the only anxieties related to survival. Health is a major concern, especially the health of you and your siblings when you are young. And of course the survival of the family as a unit is seldom not present in the thoughts of parents. A great many arguments and squabbles have to do with these concerns:

What! The washing machine broke again!
What! You bet $25 on the office football pool!
What! But we just bought you these sneakers a
month ago and now they're worn out.
What! Another visit to the doctor?

You may get the impression your parents are tight-fisted, penny-pinching and stingy, the way they go around turning out lights. Not that the few extra cents wasted on a lamp being left on needlessly will break them (and they know that), but their behavior is designed, unconsciously, to conserve and to preserve. And in their activity, they feel they are doing something useful and important. Paradoxically, while they may rant about the half-drunk can of soda left by you to fizzle and flatten out, your father may consume a six-pack of beer in the evening. Or your parents may go out for the evening and blow $50.

2) Which brings us to our next mode of behavior, the highly choreographed and ritualized social dance they do when with others. Of course you're familiar with *company manners.* After all, it's from your parents that you learn it's important to behave more politely and act differently when with people outside the family. (And then they turn around and accuse you of doing the same thing, of being civil and considerate with your friends while you're rude and sulking at home.) Have you ever noticed how your parents behave when they entertain at home? Relatives don't count. They're members of the family and can be treated the same crusty way you treat each other. But with friends they're different—deferential, cordial, poised, sophisticated, charming, perhaps even phony. Unless their relationship is far gone, on the verge of breaking up, they are likely to present a united and loving front to others,

trying to portray the picture that they are the ideal married couple, sensitive to one another's needs, attentive to each other's conversation, and supportive. Or maybe they are the "liberated" married couple, flirting with other spouses, jocular, sensuous, all very "innocent." If that's the case, then you've probably heard their post-mortems, either when the party's over or the morning after. These confrontations are not so pleasant, usually punctuated with a fair amount of acrimony and accusation.

> You had no time for me last night. The way you fawned over Jim (Jane) was enough to make me sick. You made an ass out of yourself and embarrassed me.

> You're overreacting. Just because I spent a little time with him (her) doesn't mean a thing. Why can't you understand? Don't be so jealous, especially of such an innocent thing.

> Innocent? They way you staggered around. Don't tell me you weren't three sheets to the wind when you spilled the veal into your lap. And he (she) was so *good* and *kind* as to help you clean your lap.

> At least he (she) tried to help. Which is more than I got from you. I saw your dirty look and so did everyone else. And for your information, I wasn't drunk.

("Social drinking" is another of those "social graces" that punctuate your parents' world. A little too much liquor, a slight loss of inhibition, a mild orgy.)

When they go to the local PTA meeting they are conscientious and committed. Over the backyard fence your father exchanges typical male banter with another father about how "the wife" spends too much money in department stores, about the Yankees, about how you kids are driving him crazy with your insolence. And your mother, over coffee with a neighbor at the kitchen table, talks about George spending too little time with her and how they're planning to go to Jamaica this winter and how you kids are driving her crazy with your insolence. So, together and apart, they try to create the image that they are the typical American family with normal American concerns and worries, that they have normal American aspirations for themselves, and normally insolent kids.

Listen closely and you will hear that most of it is idle chit-chat and gossip. Their talk and their actions have very little to do with anything important—with their real worries and concerns. Seldom if ever do you hear your father saying publicly, "I can't take it any longer. My mind is exploding with all the Goddamned worry and pressure. I want out. I feel I want to run away." But we bet he's thought it more than once! Nor would we expect that your mother would state at a dinner party that she felt so depressed all the time that she wanted to cry, but wouldn't for fear that if she started crying she'd never stop. She wouldn't say this, though she probably has felt it, because her "friends" would react with horror and withdraw from her, saying to themselves that she had cracked. Why? Most likely because she, in her confession, would have come too close to their own precarious situations.

The "dance" has a lot to do with appearance and illusion and with a hiding of reality. We all fear that if we speak the naked truth to one another, our world would fall apart and we would be ostracized and made outcasts. Adults often fondly comment on the child's naive ability to say what's on his mind, how the child has not learned not to tell Uncle Joe that he doesn't like him. In *The Emperor's New Clothes*, it is the child who points out that the Emperor is wearing only his pink dimpled flesh. There is nothing remarkable or insightful or naive in this behavior of the child. He is only saying what he sees and thinks and feels. He hasn't learned yet to suppress the truth. But he will—by the time he is grown up, mature, worldly. *When an adult is plagued with nightmares every night, insecure in his work, and unhappy at home, he will talk about the Yankees and his new Buick.*

3) Dominant in the romance and honeymoon are the needs for *attachment*—closeness, affection, intimacy. Though these needs wane, they never are completely suppressed in either your father or mother and continually rise up, especially at times of stress. Usually the wife, in our culture, is more expressive of these needs and their lack of fulfillment than the husband. But though husbands are seemingly more stoical and indifferent to affection, they are really just more devious and, when it comes right down to it, more gutless in having to be so devious! At such times, when your parents are tender with each other, family life is blissful and, as you have most likely noticed, there is a notable lack of tension in all of you. Things seem to go along smoothly. And there is a calm that is warm and comforting but nevertheless a trifle uneasy. For no matter how serene the state, you and the others sense that it is transitory and likely soon to fade.

This is because few of us seem able to tolerate sustained closeness. As much as we need attachment and affection, we recoil from it when we have had it for too long. Paradoxically, we tend to distance ourselves from that which we most cherish. So the seeds of distancing begin to germinate in the warmth of closeness.

4) Which leads us to that fourth, most painful, abhorred, repellent mode of behavior of marrieds which, unfortunately, is most characteristic of married life: the many behaviors of *distancing.* Classically expressed in the quarrel or argument, but also equally and poignantly expressed in a quiet emptiness, these behaviors, in moderation, help to sustain, rather than destroy, a relationship. Looked at microscopically, each quarrel seems to have a reason of its own. Who among us, after all, would think that we would want to quarrel just for the sake of quarreling? Each parent feels justified: some slight, some rudeness or inconsiderateness, some oversight, some abrasive habit known to irritate the other seems to precipitate the quarrel. Often it is a repetitive theme. For couples tend to play out their arguments around the same repetitive themes with only a limited number of variations. We bet that without too much thinking, you can come up with those themes most important to your parents. The arguments, themselves, are often bitter. When you were young they frightened you and maybe you even felt responsible for them. Now, with a long history behind you and them, you probably view them with a somewhat jaundiced eye. You may consider parents crazy to fight constantly over the same petty things and you are, in part, right. For their fighting often has a petty and petulant ring to it and at times seems to be downright childish. Although you may no longer fear that they will separate, you are disgusted with their cyclical infantile behavior, sick of it, and you want to be free of it. You are making a mistake, however, when you think your parents are more childish than others and engage in more stupid, traumatizing arguments. They have, believe it or not, good company and a lot of competition from their neighbors in Wichita and Washington.

In arguing, your parents do regress to a younger, more childlike state, a state in which, whatever the apparent issues, they are actually expressing those basic, life-sustaining needs which are not being met. And though they may try to address their complaints with specific, legitimate, mature reasoning, they cannot do this completely successfully because of the primitive, raw nature of the unmet need. So it comes out silly, acrid, painful and damaging.

But as we have said, such quarreling does—in moderation—sustain a relationship. As a violent summer thunderstorm that blackens the sky terrifies with lightning and booming thunder, and pelts the earth with savage rain, and clears and cleans the environment, so *a quarrel can often clear and cleanse the tension between your parents.*

Far worse, in our estimation, is when your parents "distance" each other by sarcastic innuendo and silence. Some parents seem seldom or never to fight with one another. They are so busy maintaining a pseudomutuality and pseudo-peace that they cannot and will not allow any rancor to come between them. They tend to nurture their grudges in silence, seeking to placate one another, rather than have it out with one another. Perhaps one of your parents is belligerent, the other subservient and submissive. Things can seem to go along well and maybe a working harmony can indeed exist for a number of years or even decades. But at a heavy price: the loss of a live, working alliance between the two. If one partner is "treating" the other, or if both are "treating" one another,* then the two can never make a decent resolution of their

---

*Whether it's good treatment or bad treatment, it's still treatment. Parents need to be loved by each other; if they need "treatment" they should go to a therapist.

differences or creatively grow within their relationship. In silence, each may kill the other and the two may effectively stifle what potential life they might have had.

The four modes of behavior that we have described reflect the life of most marrieds. (Being physicians we reserve the right, of course, to hedge on saying the absolute, and reserve, as an exception, a marriage that was truly made in heaven. While we haven't met one of those yet, we do accept, on faith, that it is possible for such a blessed union to exist.) **These conservative, socially ritualized, attaching, distancing behaviors are normative. That is, to be expected in part or whole in most marriages and, in themselves, not destructive or pathologic.**

They are the facts of married life.

11

Further Program Notes (When Things Get Out Of Hand)

You may get the impression from the preceding chapter that anything goes in marriage and that nothing has any real consequence because everybody's doing it. This is far from the truth. While in a decent, "happy" and sustained marital relationship, there is much bickering and discontent and unhappiness, such expressions have to them a certain propriety that keeps them within bounds and doesn't let them get out of hand. When things do get out of hand, then married people tend to pull away from one another, the cement of their relationship begins to crumble and crack, and things fall apart. When this happens it is altogether different from the normative "social dances" and quarrels that we have described above, and far more serious. And of course it has a much more devastating effect on you.

We will portray with thumbnail sketches certain serious conditions affecting marriages. Our list is not all-inclusive; nor is our discussion thorough and comprehensive. But perhaps we can give you some useful perspective if you live in a family in such a state of crisis.

Separation and Divorce

Just as two people can fall in love, so they can fall out of love, really fall out of love. Not the normal and expected spats, the routine dissatisfactions and dislikes, but really growing to dislike one another very cruelly. It is deciding that the other, whom one initially revered and admired and placed on a pedestal, is wrong, self-centered, not beautiful, valueless. Love is slowly eroded and replaced by hate. For a while, in the dissolution of the marriage, *hate* becomes the cement that binds the two. And hate sustains them in their fights and arguments, which become more vicious, unyielding and malignant.

It might be that hate is equally shared by both partners, or maybe it is felt more intensely by one. There is a desire to be freed from the tensions, humdrum, shackles, corrosive, debilitating limitations placed by the other. And there is a retreat into selfishness.

> *I* can't take it any longer.
> *I* am being destroyed.
> *I* want my freedom.
> *I* can't take his (her) brutality.
> *I* can be loved by someone else better.
> *I* can give love to someone else better.

The spouse is loathed, hated. And the children are shunted to the periphery—often with rationalization (which may turn out to be correct):

> They'd be better off if we separate. Our constant
>   fights are worse on them than a divorce.
> I've got to get them away from him (her).
> I've got my own life to live. Somehow they'll
>   survive.

And you find yourself caught squarely in the middle, maybe feeling like a Vietnamese peasant who walked smack into the middle of a battle between the Vietcong and the U. S. Army. You really don't want to be there. You really wish the war would stop—or at least go someplace else—so that you and your family wouldn't be killed and wouldn't have your hut destroyed and could get on with your own domestic fighting. You think that you might be able to stop the whole mess if you waved and shouted and pleaded, but you nearly get your head shot off in trying. Most likely you have equal sympathy—or lack of it—for both sides. Even if you do favor one parent's position over the other, you are bound to be torn on the inside. Even if you hate your father and secretly or openly cheer on your mother for finally standing up to him, you are bound to be affected by the loss of love you once had for him and by the hate that now replaces it.

So you and your brothers and sisters find yourselves— like the Vietnamese peasants who are caught in a war not of their making—caught in the entangling web of the emotions of your parents. You are bitter and disillusioned about that which you once believed was eternal, unalterable and steadfast...your parents' relationship and the integrity of your family which is now falling to pieces. You hate. You wish to get away from them. And you feel depressed and guilty.

Often adolescents, and sometimes even younger children, pretend that their parents' split has no effect on them.

> I couldn't care less. I'm not home that much anymore.
> It's nice to have some peace in the house.
> Why should it matter to me? They can do what they want with their lives.

If you're in this situation, don't make this mistake. Maybe if you need to save face, you can pretend to others that it's no big deal, or that nothing has really changed anyway. But *have at least one friend in whom you can confide.* And, above all else, do *be honest with yourself and feel the pain rather than bury it.* For it *does* matter to you and it *is* a big deal in your life. *And you are more likely to heal the emotional wounds sooner and more completely if you don't try to hide them.*

Anyway, you can't hide the wounds from yourself and thus ignore them. Young people who try to do this tend to become very embittered and cynical about all of life. And many tend to lose interest in things that once were important to them, like school and the future. And many tend to get into hard drugs or give up on life in other ways.

So realize, if your parents are going through a separation or divorce, that it is going to be a hell of a rough time for you. And don't make light of it. Share those feelings with your brothers and sisters. Try to band together, to save whatever you can. If there are people within the family—like grandparents or a favorite uncle or cousin—confide in them. Ask for their help and support. And don't be afraid to ask for the support of your friends, teachers and neighbors. They won't think you're a nuisance. Rather they're likely to respect you for your forthrightness and honesty.

Infidelity

Chances are pretty high—if all the sociological surveys done in the last 20 years are at all accurate—that one or both of your parents has had an extramarital sexual relationship. Conservatively it has repeatedly been estimated that this is the case for well over half of all married males and slightly less for married females. It may be that the relationship was isolated, casual, a one-night stand. Perhaps it was the by-product of a business trip to another city and acted on out of loneliness, or adventure, or too much alcohol. Or it may be that one has had a series of casual short-term relationships with no obvious interest other than the gratification of sexual desire. Or it may be that the relationship was or is sustaining over a period of time, an actual affair with interest and affection, perhaps even love, as an important part of the relationship.

It may be that the unfaithful parent is completely discreet in his (her) extramarital relationship and that the other parent never has an inkling of what is going on. Or the other may have some suspicion deriving from a seeming change in mood, maybe being a bit preoccupied, spending a lot of time at the "office" or "PTA meeting," a lessening of sexual ardor at home. Or it may be that the parent is only partially discreet and that some people other than the spouse know what's going on, people who may gossip or even drop hints to the spouse. Or it may be that one is completely indiscreet and doesn't care who knows and flaunts the relationship even to the spouse.

It may be that the infidelity is harmless and has no effect on the marital relationship whatsoever. (Some marital therapists believe that for certain couples, an extramarital relationship can even have a positive effect on a marriage.) Or it may be that the affair(s) is devastating and destructive and leads to the parents getting divorced. Sometimes one parent will divorce the other for another woman (man). Sometimes simply to be "free."

100

Thus you can see that infidelity has many faces and runs the gamut from the inconsequential to the highly significant. The more innocuous it is, the less you are likely to know about it. The more it affects your parents' relationship, the more you will be involved. You might sense it in some argument between your parents overheard by you or you might be struck in the face by an outright accusation at the dinner table or by one parent leaving the other.

Infidelity does weaken the bond between two people. It does cause some damage between parents even when it is utterly "discreet" in that it lessens the sense of intimacy and places in the mind of one a *secret* to be kept from the other. And when suspected or known, it is seen as a violation of trust between the two. Thus, it is *never* innocent even when it is seen as most "innocent."

Why is one person unfaithful to another? Why does one cheat on another? Again there are many reasons, none of them mutually exclusive. One may tire of the other, be bored and feel locked into a dreary relationship. Usually under the boredom, there is another powerful emotion—*anger*—which may or may not be perceived by the individual. One is angry with the other for doing this or not doing that, for some real or imagined grievance, for some legitimate or false sense that one's needs are not being met. And one uses the boredom and anger as justification for being with another: "If I can't get it (sex, love, attention, respect) at home, I'll get it elsewhere."

Another set of reasons has to do with the "seven year itch." It is common for one to feel bogged down even in a good relationship and to somehow feel cheated by being monogamous or feel that life is sliding by as he (she) ages. Especially today, if one listens to and believes all the soap operas, the situation comedies and melodramas on TV and the movies, the message of the flesh magazines and the frankly provocative sexual themes of so many advertisements, one can feel almost like a fool for being monogamous! People in their late 30's and 40's who are beginning to get paunchy and to wrinkle and creak, people like your parents, are especially susceptible to these media messages. "What's it like," they ask themselves, "to be with somebody else? How do I know that I'm not missing out on something great?...Well, I'd better get it before it's too late." For a grown person, presumably in a stable marriage, to fall in love again is to recapture some emotion from the past, the overpowering feeling—breathless and all-consuming—of finding another so irresistible, exciting, glamorous, that one thinks of no one and nothing else. So, as important as this other person may be or seem to be, the *feeling* is more important to the individual for it is a link to his (her) lost youth when he (she) had such emotions frequently. In finding these emotions again, brought out by the other person, one pushes back one's own clock, forestalls advancing middle-age, and is young again...or seems to be.

And so off they go, sometimes without thinking, and embark on some adventure which they may later regret. In sex, as in everything else, we all tend to think that we're missing out on something, that somewhere else, with someone else, life could be grander, richer, more exciting. Sad to say, the grass is usually not greener, often not as green. But that's not something we are likely to know unless we've been there.

Alcoholism

How do you know when your parent has been drinking too much? When your father comes home from work and has two stiff scotches, is he merely unwinding from a hard day at the office—as so many fathers do—or is he addicted to alcohol and drinking too heavily? What about your mother? Is she sipping sherry in the afternoon, and is this something to worry about? Have your parents pushed back the "drinking hour" earlier and earlier as the years go by? Do one or both of them come home drunk from parties? Do they often have hangovers, and is it any concern of yours?

It is difficult to pinpoint exactly when a person passes over the line from social drinking into alcoholism. And it is hard to know when he begins to depend on alcohol to get through the day and uses it to quell and soothe his frustrations. Certainly such a person is not going to be the first to recognize it. Usually the alcoholic is the last in his family or job or social group to realize and admit he has a problem. It is the others around the problem drinker who recognize it first and have the painful and awkward responsibility of trying to convince the person that he has a problem and had better get help for it.

Alcoholics tend to deny that they have a drinking problem and are likely to act insulted if you suggest it. They respond with one or more of the following (after telling you it's none of your business):

I like to drink and can hold my drink...look! I can walk a straight line.
I drink because I'm happy, sad, angry, upset, excited, euphoric, worried, under a lot of pressure..:Besides it tastes good.
If I didn't have to put up with your nagging and always letting me down, I wouldn't have to drink so much.

It doesn't interfere with my work. And it makes
   me better able to tolerate all the tension at
   home.
Are you saying I'm a skid row bum? If you think
   I'm bad, what about your Uncle Charlie?
All right. So I'm an alcoholic... Throw me in jail.

And the major mistake that many families of alcoholics
make is to play along with the drinker, placating him,
trying to prevent him from getting upset, covering up for
him, looking the other way, laughing at his antics and ex-
ploits, hiding his booze, pouring it down the sink, water-
ing it down. In other words they do everything but face it
squarely and help him to face it squarely.

**If you suspect that a parent is drinking too much, have
the guts to talk about it with your other parent.** Let's say,
for example, that you've smelled alcohol on your
mother's breath most afternoons when you've come
home from school for the last six months. Occasionally
she looks a little tipsy, seldom slurs her speech, but is un-
usually tired lately and sleeping a lot in the afternoon. It
appears to you that the house has not been quite so
neatly kept as it used to be and, while the meals are on
the table, they're not up to the usual quality of the past.
Your mother's moods are more mercurial. She and dad
seem to drink a lot more in the evening and have little to
say to one another except for some silly domestic quarrel
that she initiates.

In summary, Mom seems different. You can't quite put
your finger on it except for the alcohol on her breath. So
you go to talk with your Dad. If he's responsive, if he con-
fides in you that he, too, has been concerned and has suspected that she's drinking too much, then half the battle's
won. But if he tells you you're silly and admonishes you

not to talk such nonsense about your mother, don't give up. *First try to observe, more closely, and carefully, how much she drinks and what her patterns of drinking are.* Obviously the more booze and the more of the day consumed with boozing, the greater the likelihood of a problem. *Second, talk with others and get their opinion.* Though you may feel like a rat and a betrayer of your mother, if you do it sincerely, you're much more likely to be of help in the long run. See what your family doctor or minister thinks. (By the way, many ministers are quite up on the signs and problems of alcoholism and quite adept in giving advice and counsel.) *Or go to your local Al-Anon Chapter (a branch of Alcoholics Anonymous for relatives of an alcoholic).* Tell them your story. Get their advice. See how they can help your father to realize your mother's illness so the two of you can confront her and get her help.

Above all, don't coddle her. Or pretend that she doesn't have a problem if you think she does have one. It won't do her any good. Nor will it do you any good. For alcoholism is a disease that affects others as much as it affects the alcoholic. It can lead to much family unhappiness or even broken homes. If the alcoholic loses his job, then the whole family income and finances may be shot. So bite the bullet. You and other members of the family have got to confront and deal with the denial until you get your point across and your parent accepts the fact that he or she has a drinking problem.

By the way, we would give the same advice to your parents if they suspected that you had a problem with drugs or alcohol. There's nothing to be gained by pretending it doesn't exist if it does.

Job Jumping, Absenteeism

When the family breadwinner plays around with his job, not only does he endanger himself, but he endangers the whole family. He may hate his job or have conflict with his boss. He may feel that he's been slighted and passed over for promotion. He may get no personal satisfaction from his work and wish that he had another job. If he carefully looks for another job, weighs the merits and drawbacks of that new job compared with his present one, then he is acting in a responsible manner. Of course, there isn't necessarily anything pathologic about seeking and getting a new job. Indeed to stay in a lousy job is in itself something to really get concerned about!

But sometimes breadwinners behave irresponsibly. While skipping work and calling in sick is very fashionable nowadays, it's not a good practice and certainly doesn't set a good example for you. *People seldom, if ever, deal successfully with conflict by avoidance.* It's sort of like playing hookey from school. It may feel good for an hour or two, but if you're at all concerned about getting an education, then you've got to wonder what it was you missed and worry about whether you can make it up. It's no different on the job. People notice. The one who's absent gets a reputation that he's not able to be relied upon. And he gets passed over. If he uses up all his sick days and then gets really sick, his whole family suffers.

Same thing goes with job-hopping. Some people go from job to job every couple of years. They find something major wrong with every job they have. They feel they never get a fair shake. They are constantly disappointed in their search. They leave for something better only to find it's no better. And sometimes they uproot their family from city to city. Obviously such individuals are focusing all of the dissatisfactions with all aspects of life onto the job.

Usually there are other important concerns and problems which get pushed aside by the job issue.

Excessive Debts

Almost all American families live beyond their means. With the easy availability of credit cards, installment buying and bank loans, it's relatively painless for most families to buy a $6000 car (after all it's only $99 a month for 48 months after a down payment which can probably be borrowed too). Likewise vacations, clothes, dishwashers, home improvements, entertainment, almost anything you can think of, can be charged. And today, with our crazy economy and spiraling inflation, even frugal families have to live beyond their means. Nothing is cheap anymore but money.

But some families really do live excessively and dangerously beyond their means. They have to have the latest this and the newest that. They never seem to have enough of what they need (whatever that is) and feel that new possessions and acquisitions, superior material goods, will enhance and enrich their lives. They spend and buy as if there were no tomorrow.

Until tomorrow comes. The house is heavily mortgaged. The savings account is empty and a personal check bounces. Meanwhile the friendly bank and credit card company are breathing down their necks and the roof springs a leak and the heater breaks down. Boy! What a tomorrow!

Such families usually try to gratify non-material needs with material goods. And it just doesn't work.

Gambling And Other Reckless Behavior

It's one thing to put $10 into an office football pool or take out a weekly lottery ticket or go to the racetrack occasionally. But it's another thing to want to bet on almost everything that comes along, to skip work to go to the racetrack, to bet $50 on one round of golf, to play cards compulsively. And to lose.

There's a breed of person who's a compulsive gambler, the sort of person for whom gambling is a way of life, as much of an addiction as alcohol is for the alcoholic. Such an individual thinks he gambles to win. He usually gambles with money he either doesn't have or which should be used for something else. He's always trying to beat the system. And he is the delight of the professional gambler, the racetrack, the casino, because he is a loser over the long haul. His addiction is destructive to himself and others and is suicidal.

There are many other ways that adults can flirt with death short of outright committing suicide. They can eat way too much and clog their arteries. Or after a heavy meal and out of shape, they can put on their new sweatsuit and jog around the block. You can think of the many ways they try, physically, to act as if they were 20 rather than 45.

Likewise they can drive fast and very aggressively, sky dive, downhill ski, and scuba dive. A friend of ours once hunted jaguar in Guatemala armed only with a flashlight. The trick was to make contact with the jaguar at night in the jungle, have it pick up his scent and then beat it—beat it back to camp before the jaguar could get him!

We humans have strange ways of defying and courting death at the same time. You may detect that an implicit theme runs through the subjects of this chapter. And that is the theme of our *mortality*. Your parents are never far removed from some kind of preoccupation with time running out in their lives. They are, after all, on the downhill slope. The days and years are shorter and go faster. Sometimes they act as if they wanted to turn back the clock or to stop it. At other times their behaviors seem to suggest that they'd as soon turn it ahead to meet the inevitable. There are some strange things adults do in the name of maturity. Claiming to be in conscious control of their actions, nevertheless they seem to be driven by forces of which they are unaware. What is the nature and the origin of these forces?

Mental Illness

There's a considerable difference between everyday "crazy" or "sick" behavior, or people's superstitions or "hangups," and mental illness. When someone "freaks out" or "crashes," or goes into a rage, that person is then mentally ill because he is not accountable for his behavior which is no longer under his rational control. Just about everyone has these moments of insanity (we say "everyone," but we don't know everyone), which ordinarily pass quickly and are accepted as part of daily life—just something that you and they have to put up with. But when periods of irrationality, or elation, or depression, go on for weeks or months, or sometimes even years, with measurable changes in the way the brain computes as well as in body chemistry, then we may appropriately use the term *mental illness*.

If someone in your family has a mental illness, the great probability is that, in time, they'll get well enough to function as they did before—and we realize that this is not exactly the same as saying they'll get over the illness completely, although they probably will get completely over this particular episode: they may have a recurrence. On the other hand, if someone is a mental defective ("feeble-minded") or if an older person becomes senile, you should not expect them to get over it. So there are two kinds of mental illness: reversible and irreversible.

If one of your parents becomes mentally ill, it is vital that this be recognized as quickly as possible so that that person, and perhaps the whole family, may get the treatment that is required. Otherwise there is a good chance that several lives will be destroyed.

There are two important things that you need to know about mental illness in one of your parents. First, *you* did not cause it, and second, *you* cannot cure it.

But how should you behave toward a parent in that condition? Our answer is that you must act in an absolutely clear, uncomplicated, straightforward manner. No tricks, no clever subtleties, no attempts to manipulate the situation. Because the sick person's brain is not computing in its usual way. This behavior on your part isn't curative in itself, but it may keep things from getting worse, and it may help the curative forces of nature.

Now you may feel that before your parent became diagnosably ill, he or she was rather tricky and confusing him- or herself, and played a number of mischievous or even vicious games with you and others. *It may help for you to think of these "games" as that person's attempt to stave off mental illness. It may also be helpful to think of much parental misbehavior—gambling, drinking, marital infidelity, and so on—as an attempt, a futile, misguided attempt, to hold on to sanity.*

When people are under stress they may break down in a number of ways. One way, of course, is to break down physically, as by getting an ulcer or by having a heart attack, or simply by getting so run down that their resistance is low and they fall easy victim to a virus or a bacterium or even a fungus or mold. But some people don't get physically ill very easily, and their moral code is so strong that they don't misbehave, and they may go from apparent health directly into mental illness—but it only seems that way to another person because they can't see the conflict and turmoil that's going on inside the sufferer.

We think that a number of people have very warped attitudes about mental illness. Some make fun of it or act as though the mentally ill are faking. Some people nowadays say that there is no mental illness. Without getting into all of the relevant arguments, we would like to point out that there are many, many people who are diagnosably severely neurotic or psychotic, and that they and many others are undergoing extreme mental or emotional anguish because of this. Many others are very frightened of mental illness in themselves or in members of their family, or in anyone, and no doubt they would be much relieved if they could talk or laugh it out of existence. We guess you know how we feel about that!

Physical Illness

Yes, parents do become physically ill because of emotional stress, but there are other reasons for physical illness. First of all, some physical disorders are hereditary. Certain endocrine or glandular disorders, such as diabetes, are genetically determined. So are certain kinds of blindness and deafness, and many other disorders. Some adult illnesses are the result of birth defects which are not mapped out in the genes, but which result from diseases or other problems associated with pregnancy or with the birth process. Third, some people are exposed to powerful microorganisms, as during epidemics, and their natural resistance does not include the appropriate antibodies. Fourth, there are injuries which may result in a parent being permanently crippled in some way, such as by being paralyzed or blinded. Finally, some people's bodily parts just wear out faster than others for no apparent reason. Scattered among the preceding are such disparate particulars as cancer, poison and attempted murder.

So people do have physical illnesses, and your parents doubtless have had them, have them, or will get them. And as we pointed out in the last section, you didn't *cause* them and you can't *cure* them, although it is possible for you to have been involved in causing an injury to one of them, even as, tragically, they may have injured you. But don't get any fantasies about operating on your grandmother and removing her brain tumor; let someone else do it. (On the other hand, if you want to find a cure for cancer or for heart disease, don't let us discourage you!)

If a parent has physical problems, he or she may or may not want help from one or more of their adolescent children. Similarly, you may feel a strong need to help your parent; on the other hand, you may not. This is explainable and understandable on the basis of rational, conscious motives, but there are also powerful *unconscious* forces operating on both sides resulting in attitudes not so easily grasped. For example, a parent may want help because he knows he needs it and is willing to accept that need. On the other hand, his physical need may not be so great, but his emotional dependency needs are triggered by a relatively minor disability, and he might regress to a state of infantile helplessness! Or he may refuse help because objectively he simply can manage without it, or he may turn it down because he is "too proud"—but this may be simply a way of saying he is unwilling to give up his control, his accustomed role of parental authority, which he might have to relinquish partially if he lets you feel indispensable.

For your part, you may not want to help because you can't bear thinking of a parent as weakened, or out of hostile feelings toward him, or because you know it's not good for him to get dependent, or because you consider it unwise to give up school to take a job, or give up your social life to stay home with your mother, and on and on. Conversely you may want to help because it's right and proper, because you're willing to be sucked in by your parent's dependency, or because you want an excuse to avoid social competition, or because you're covering up hostile feelings, or denying your own dependency needs, and on and on.

It is certainly safe to say that there are a large number of ways your parent can handle the situation produced by his own illness, and there are a number of ways in which you may respond to any move by your parent. The important corollary of these contingencies is that each pairing of what your parent does and what you do has an outcome that is different from all the others. *It's something to think about: there's a lot more to physical illness than just physical illness!*

Part IV

THE UNFINISHED BUSINESS
OF ADOLESCENCE
(IT'LL COME BACK TO HAUNT YOU)

It is very difficult to give up adolescence and become an adult. There are not only pleasures to be foregone as responsibilities are acquired; there are also ideals, dreams and aspirations that must be filed away, possibly for future use. Most of what is filed may never be used, but two very dramatic things do happen. In the first place, in what seems superficially to be a most mysterious manner, the dreams are passed on to the adolescent children of the parents, who are at least temporarily freed from having to actualize them (the Adult Moratorium). The second thing that happens is that the adolescent relives situations similar to what his parent experienced; this has a most startling effect on the parent!

12

The Second Identity Crisis:
I. The First Identity
Crisis Revisited

What does it mean to grow up? What does it mean to mature? And what changes go on, must go on, as one matures? Was it really possible for your parents, at the age of 14, fully to conceive of what they would be like at the age of 24 (at 18 did they have a clearer picture of 28 or at 35 of what it would be like to be 45)? For while they may have had expectations, dreams of what they wanted to be and to do, images of how they'd like to act and relate to others, dreams of how they wanted to look and dress, they could have had no clear idea of what changes would take place within them over the next critical and formative decade. What would they have to give up to grow up, and were they ready and prepared to give it up? Perhaps they were mentally ready and willing to give up their parents, but were they fully emotionally prepared to do this? They may well have felt that their parents were a burden and a straightjacket, a source of much frustration, irritation and emotional pain. They may on occasion have even seen them stand in the way of attaining maturity and independence. But were they really capable, at this point, of writing off their parents and going it alone?

What is involved in developing the mental, emotional and physical strength to stand on one's own two feet?

And how does one go about getting it? Is there something that one has to do, some secret cipher that must be decoded to gain this strength? Is there any way the process can be hastened? Or is there little or nothing to be done? Should one just sit back and allow oneself to be floated, naturally and effortlessly, into maturity?

These are a few of the many questions that in one way or another your parents must have been asking themselves. We want to explore in this chapter some of what is involved in the process of growing up, some of what one gains as one ages, and what one loses, or leaves behind.

The landmarks of maturation are fairly obvious. It's just the navigation to them that is mysterious and clouded. First, in our culture, maturation is associated with leaving home, with effecting a more or less amicable separation from one's family. (By the way, the more amicable and mutually supported the separation, the better are the chances for survival and mastery in the world. People who run away from home or leave with acrimony, bitterness, and hate, tend to have a rough time of it. They seem unable to shake the unhappiness and the pain of that experience. While those who make some kind of personal and emotional peace before leaving home are better able to make a go of it.)

Along with separation, an equally important psychological task is the development of an independent sense of self, a constant and abiding sense of personal identity. Now, *identity* is a fancy and popular term, used a lot by all of us as we seek to define ourselves. But your parents asked, at age 14, didn't they have it then? (Did you have it then?) They knew who they were, where they lived and where they went each day. But people are changeable. Passions are often mercurial and values possibly vacillate

over a wide range. And if they thought closely, they may
have found much inner mistrust, misgivings and igno-
rance about themselves. If they were like most people,
they tended to shy away from this sort of introspection,
for it tends to breed anxiety and further insecurity.* If
they could accept that they didn't yet have a wholeness,
an identity, how would they get it? And can one ever get
it? It's a frightening thought, but the odds are greatly in
favor of one's getting this stable self-concept, and without
having to go to a psychiatrist for counseling.

Other landmarks may be reached from these two central ones. With inner strength and stability, one naturally
tends to look to the future, to chart directions and set educational, vocational and social goals for oneself. One
gets into the right school (for him or her), and picks a
course that both stimulates intellectually and prepares
one for the future. When one's education is completed,
having terminated at high school or college or graduate
school, as the case may be, one is ready for a vocation
that will bring financial rewards, security, personal satisfaction and that will also allow some professional growth.
Socially, gradually one finds his own level in life, his own
Karma, and gains a circle of friends with whom comfort,
happiness and good times are to be found. Of course,

---

*Introspection is the art or practice of exploring what is in your mind
or how your mind works. This (inner space) has traditionally been the
domain of philosophers, Oriental and Mid-Eastern mystics, and 19th
and early 20th century experimental psychologists, but anyone can
look inward upon himself and investigate his ideas and images, his
feelings and sensations. For most action-oriented people, introspection can be a valuable balance wheel to keep them in touch with
themselves. For those people who tend to wallow in their own psyche,
however, it can produce problems; perhaps for them more action
would provide a good balance!

from this circle one picks out the one most special—with whom we are most comfortable—who becomes one's spouse. This all seems easy enough, once it has been done successfully, maybe not as ridiculously easy as we have described it, but still easy enough (to think about).

But the doing of it, that's another thing: a struggle filled with uncertainty and vacillation, a striving for survival flooded in a torrent of anxiety. So it was for your parents, and their parents before them. As they tell you about their adolescent experiences—how they did this and that, how they went to sock-hops and danced cheek to cheek and sang along with Nat "King" Cole and Frank Sinatra, how they chug-a-lugged beer and dared one another to play "chicken" in their open convertibles, how they cheered as their basketball team won or lost the championship game, how they went steady with someone different every month, how they were able to be more intent in their studies because life was much clearer and more structured (in those days they questioned and argued with authorities less than young people do today)—and when you see their golden age on TV or in the movies—how the Fonz has a boyishness and goofy nonchalance about life, how Bogie, in one picture after another, seems always to get the bad guy and the good gal, how clean-cut the girls were in their pleated skirts and bobby-sox and the boys in their crew cuts and wide smiles—it all seems terribly nostalgic and romantic…and dated. And unreal, much more of a myth than a reality. For as we age most of us tend to forget, or minimize, or put aside the bad memories, the troublesome experiences and stupid actions of our youth. When occasionally we remember what was conflict-producing, it may still evoke a sudden, disquieting chill within us, a flush of nervousness, an inner embarrassment and discomfort that seems to rise up from nowhere and to haunt us. So we try not to think about those things, about how we didn't really know what we were doing and where we were going; and we think only of the good things in the "good old days." And that is how we, as parents, tend to construct a mythic picture of our past, based more on our distortions, reconstructions and reshapings of what happened than on what really happened. And that is what we, as parents, tend to pass on to you.

It was so easy, so graceful, so effortless! And if you believe in the myth, intimidating to you. What went wrong, you may ask, between your parents' generation and yours? How come you seem to have so much more trouble than they? Is it, as many will say, that life is infinitely more difficult and complex now than it was then? Is it that you are less well equipped to handle life's stresses than they because: 1) You are softer, having been pampered more than they and not having had to struggle for necessities; or, 2) you are a product of the "permissive generation," your parents having given you too much too soon; or, 3) you are a member of the TV generation, your mind having been rotted by the Three Stooges and an endless sequence of Bugs Bunny cartoons, your will and strength washed away by soap, detergent, toothpaste and mouthwash commercials? Maybe you react to this intimidation by counterattack: 1) Your parents were a naive and dumb bunch. Look at their songs. While they listened to the inanities of Bing Crosby and other crooners extolling love, love lost, love gained, you were immersed in the gut verities and brutal frankness of Bob Dylan; 2) your parents had a much simpler time of it. Smaller numbers of people. Less to know. Fewer decisions to make. Didn't have to or want to think for themselves; 3) you're a much more sophisticated product than they were and are wiser, more worldly, more finely attuned to the subtler nuances of life.

But the truth is that their youth was, by and large, as difficult, confusing and troubled as yours is. While the issues are different, the underlying themes of differentiation, definition of self, and determination of direction, are identical. The reality for them was as uncertain as their constructed myth is certain, and every bit as uncertain as your reality is for you.

Then you may ask, why have they so doctored up their reality with their myth, why have they tarnished what was honest and painful with fakery and tinsel, why have they not been able to hang onto what they experienced and accept it for what it was? Probably for the same reasons that you will make myth out of your experiences, and alchemize what is real into something that is unreal.

Behind these reasons is a profound sense of *loss*, a felt sense of loss of one's youth and innocence and freshness, a loss of time and of freedom. At the age of twelve, let's say, the days pass slowly and almost too leisurely. Most likely you had much joy in your sports and other pleasures, but there was already beginning an impatience with your present lot. You were restless, eager to get on, to begin things on your own, to forge your own life. As the days and months went by, you noticed an increase, a gradual crescendo in your activity. It was as if you had been tranquilly canoeing down a calm river, satiny in its smoothness. But ahead you saw white water. As you approached it, the waters around you grew choppy and turbulent. You had less control over your craft and suddenly, as you slid into a swift current, you lost all control. You panicked, your heart climbed into your throat as you banged against a rock. But you caromed off, and passed through the whirlpool once more into calmer waters. But ahead you saw still another patch of white water. And somewhere, down river, you knew that there was a waterfall.

Like the river, adolescence is a period of turbulence alternating with a period of calm, with an increasingly dangerous current that leads to a waterfall. During the calm periods there is time for reflection and pleasure, time to plan and dream and to plot your course. But in the turbulent periods, all thought goes over the side except the one thought to survive. What has to be jettisoned will be jettisoned no matter what its immediate or potential value.

And therein, metaphorically, derives some of the loss. *To mature, one must put something aside. In the process of growing up, one must come to grips with who one is and what one is capable of.* This is sobering. It is a chilling and often disillusioning experience to face one's own limitations and to become aware of one's own mortality. If, for a moment, we think of the waterfall as marking a coming of age and that paradoxically, one must get swept over that falls in order to survive, then a special corollary paradox follows. Namely, that which is necessary for survival (that is, to be swept over the falls, to reach independence) may, in itself, be hazardous enough to cause maiming or even death (that is, one may be crushed, or drowned, in the falls, unable to get past it and reach maturity).

Once beyond the falls, once into maturity, when looking back, it is easy and all too human to minimize the experience. One is a little ashamed and embarrassed about the degree of panic one had, about how one overreacted to what was really not such a perilous or threatening journey after all. And, thus, the myth is born.

Let us go back a little way. We are proposing that what is most desired by the adolescent—maturity and independence—is, at the same time, most threatening and potentially perilous. And that, in the gaining of it, one must give up a great deal. One jettisons the security of the family, the closeness of relationships with parents and siblings, the need to be nurtured, the desire to be cared for and have everything made right, and the comfort of having a well-defined place—however dependent—under the protective supervision, the benevolent despotism, of a parent. Perhaps these beliefs are, in themselves, myths, more illusory than real, but they are powerful forces from the past, nonetheless, as one approaches the moment of truth. With no certainty that one can make the leap into adulthood, one must put aside earlier comforts. Yet they remain within the dim recesses of one's consciousness and continue to exert pulls on one through life's struggles and hassles, especially at times of extreme stress.

Second, in surging forward, *one must put aside, leave unfinished, much of the business of childhood and adolescence: the leisurely discovery of self and the conflicts with self, the conflicts with parents and others.* All these fade as one moves ahead; they are left unresolved or only partially resolved. This deficiency is not forgotten. Rather it continues to make a strong statement throughout one's adult life, often expressed as a longing to return to a simpler, calmer, less troubled time, as a yearning for serenity and peace, or as a heartache for not having healed wounds given others and for not having come *truly to understand one's parents—and thus to have forgiven them.*

Yet, finally, these fears and yearnings are put aside by most of us as our exhilaration mounts on our nearing the time of decision. Like Pascal we have the faith to make a blind leap in the dark, hoping, wishing, praying that what we leave behind will be more than made up for by what we will gain on reaching adulthood. For along with our fears and trepidations, we discover much excited anticipation about what lies ahead for us. It is as if we stand on the threshold of an utterly new and unique experience. As in watching *The Wizard of Oz*, we see Dorothy's (that is, our) childhood in black and white and the world of expectation, dream, fantasy, in blazing technicolor. We experience an elation that is actually heightened by the danger and uncertainty. The world is waiting for us to come and get it. Just as there is no love quite so poignant as the first love one experiences in adolescence, so is the time of emerging adulthood imbued with a sense of high adventure that we may never experience again no matter how successful we are in life, no matter how high we climb.

And so, **in reaching for our future, we put aside our past.** We may believe that we do this once and for all, but we will get back to it again, slightly jaded by our experiences, with hopes not realized, with dreams compromised and perhaps even turned into nightmares, wearied by defeat and the hard battle to keep our heads above water. And we get back to it, curiously, as our own children reach into adolescence and head to their own moments of truth.

13

The Second Identity Crisis:
II. The Adult Moratorium

There used to be a saying that adolescents are the best philosophers. This did not mean that there were a couple of kids just out of high school who had managed to figure out once and for all where the Universe originated or what its purpose is or what its fate will be, or why man is here on this earth, nor did it mean that they had discovered the formula for Beauty, or what is Good in all situations, or what are the ultimate units of knowledge, or, for that matter, how we manage to know anything at all, or even that they had invented a system of mathematical notation that can be understood by any creature that has more than two brain cells. It didn't really intend to say that they had cornered the market on any particular idea or intuition or analytic method; it did mean that adolescents, because of their special position between childhood and adulthood, being confronted with the bewildering problem of acquiring their own identity, naturally are especially curious about what kind of world they are a part of, about what *is* real and what *seems* real, about what is important and what is trivial, what is valuable and what is trash.

Adolescents, therefore, have a reason to be interested in the traditional areas of concern of philosophy. Moreover, not being committed to any system of belief, political party, or special interest group, not having any particular axe to grind, they are accordingly able to view philosophic questions with some objectivity. Finally, being full of energy and good, healthy animal spirits, they are able to present their feelings and beliefs with enthusiasm and vigor, and they are certainly not afraid to attack established positions.

There may actually be very few, if any, adolescents today who think of themselves as philosophers, or who are knowingly interested in philosophic questions, but there are certainly plenty of adolescents who know what they believe to be Good and what they believe to be Bad, and they are unquestionably ready to attack all established positions.

But, most of all, adolescents want the *Truth*. They do not want to hear any baloney, apple-crapple, or bull.

Now, as we've been trying to tell you, once upon a time, when your parents were your age, they too were seekers after Truth. Yes, difficult though it may be to imagine, these uptight defenders of the status quo were actually wishing it were a better world and that Goodness would win out over Badness, instead of vice versa, which seems usually to be the case. The reason we know this is true is that we were in the same place and most of the adults we talk to were in the same place when it was their turn to be adolescents.

Thinking about serious issues involves a certain sense of responsibility. If one gets the idea that the world *could* be better it doesn't necessarily follow that it's his responsibility to *make* it better. But the healthy adolescent tends to be action-oriented; furthermore, he is locked in mortal competition with his parents: if they are responsible for the mess the world's in, he wants to show that he can make it a better world through his own efforts. And that is probably where your parents were: wanting to make it a better world, trying to *do* something, or perhaps just talking about it, but nevertheless participating in whatever was available to them. There are many paths they may have followed to move in this direction. They may have joined the Socialist Party or they may have become Young Republicans or beatniks or vegetarians, but it really doesn't matter much which particular course they followed because, even if they merely read the Great Books, they were doing something they believed in, something they thought would make this a better life for all.

So what happened? As the late Adlai Stevenson said: "A funny thing happened to me on the way to the White House" (he lost the election). Similarly, a funny thing happened to your parents on the road to Utopia. They got sidetracked. The old biological impulse to procreate, to build nests, got the better of them. Their hormones started chugging through their arteries, carrying messages from the ancient and primitive instincts which had been programmed into their germ cells, and almost without thinking about it, they found themselves married and committed to raising children. (It's not just biological, of course; there are many, many social pressures, too.)

Maybe your dad is an insurance salesman and liked to play catch with you and was very set on getting you involved in Little League, but you know that he'd wanted to become a Big League pitcher. He played varsity ball in high school and college and even made it to a major league farm club, where he was 7-and-3 his first season. Baseball wasn't just a game to him; it wasn't even just a profession; it was a way of life. When he stood on the mound getting the sign from his catcher, he was confronting the batter, one on one, like a matador confronting *el toro* in the bull-ring in Madrid. But something happened to his arm, and he had to give up baseball. Too bad.

Maybe your mother had wanted to be a lawyer. She got good grades in high school and was active in the Debating Society and went to every civil rights meeting she could possibly attend. Her parents weren't well off financially, but she was able to get a scholarship to college. Unfortunately it was only a partial scholarship and she couldn't raise the rest of the money she needed for her freshman year. So she got a part-time job and started her first semester, but it proved to be too exhausting and she got sick and had to drop out. That's how it goes sometimes.

Or maybe your father was going to be a medical missionary; perhaps he had planned to go to Asia and start a hospital in one of the undeveloped areas of the Third World. But when he found that he had family responsibilities of his own, he decided to go into private practice in obstetrics and gynecology, and now he and some other docs have their own hospital, but it's in beautiful downtown Burbank, rather than in Bangladesh. No tragedy so far, but is this what he really wanted to be doing?

If you or someone else had asked him if this was in fact what he had in mind, his first answer might have been that he was too busy doing it to think about questions like that. His second answer might have been that of course this was what he wanted to do; look how successful he was, look at how much money he made, and look at how many people thought how wonderful he was. Maybe around the fourth or fifth answer he might have allowed that he has a tiger by the tail and that everything is OK as long as he keeps working at it, but that he can't afford to stop and look at it, neither financially nor emotionally nor intellectually, unless he wanted to have a heart attack or similar catastrophe (which people sometimes later refer to as a "blessing" because it made them look at and change their way of living).

But no matter how far you took your questions, you wouldn't hear him say that all along what he really wanted to be was a medical missionary in Bangladesh. Suppose, however, you had known that he once harbored this sort of dream, that you had seen it written in black and white under his picture in his high school yearbook, and that you confronted him with this thirty-year-old secret: what would he say then? Probably he'd be startled, incredulous, and embarrassed. Perhaps he'd say that yes, he'd thought about it, but it was a silly adolescent dream. Impractical. Something he couldn't possibly have afforded to do. How could he have married and had you kids and bought this house and the cars and the boat and joined the country club and sent you to private school and summer camp and travelled? No, it was just an adolescent dream.

But what about *then*? Wasn't the dream valid then? Well, what did he know then—about the world—about how life is—about how you have to do things...It was an attitude based on incomplete information. Naive.

So here are you at 18 and here's your dad at 48 telling you that when he was 18 he was having silly adolescent dreams! Where does that leave you?

Then you come up with your ace in the hole. You have his medical school yearbook, and you ask him if he knows what it says under his picture. This time he actually blushes! Sure enough, eight years later, at 26, he still wants to be a medical missionary! Hey, Dad, still an adolescent fantasy at age 26?

Two years later your parents got married, and two years after that you were born. Did that mean that Mom and you and the rest of the kids were also part of an adolescent fantasy? Where did it end? When did your father stop dreaming and wake up to what he calls the "realities" of life? Or is it all some kind of crazy kid dream with one part no more valid than another?

There can be no doubt that there are realities. There is no doubt that you are a reality, and there is no doubt that there are very real feelings and very real responsibilities that your dad has toward you.

And there can be no doubt that your having been born made a real difference in the way your father felt about the world and about himself. It is not impossible, indeed it is most likely, that until you were born your dad still believed in his dream—not just in its validity, but that it was actually going to come true!

But then there were doctor bills, and clothes, and nursery school and breathing lessons (you don't suppose kids come into this world knowing just how to breathe, do you?) And then your dad thought, Holy Dollar! I'd better start making money! And so there he was, off to the rat races.

Of course your dad didn't do this alone. When your mom married him there can be no doubt that she thought your father's plan to become a medical missionary was absolutely neat. She was right behind him all the way, pushing. But when she got pregnant something very subtle happened to her. Her own nest-building instinct was turned on, evoked, no doubt, by the changes in her own hormone balance, and she began murmuring things to your dad about a cozy split-level nest (he wanted a big old-fashioned plantation house with pillars and a portico).

As you grew older they became more involved in the suburban scene, and they naturally assumed that you would follow the same life course they did. They took it for granted that you would have the same values they did. They wanted you to look right, and behave properly, and get very good grades in school so that you would get into a top-ranking university and later a fine professional school. When you said you weren't interested in all that, they were aghast. What did you want to be when you grew up? You said you'd thought it over and decided that when you grew up you wanted to be an elephant. An *elephant!* How could you do this to them? How could you be like that? So frivolous, so ridiculous! If you couldn't take your future seriously what would become of you! After all they'd done for you!

Well, you *did* know what you wanted to do, but you certainly weren't going to tell *them*. You and your loved friend had decided that you wanted to have a home for runaway kids. You knew that when kids run away from home it's because the place they ran away from really isn't a home and their parents really aren't parents. So the two of you would set up a home, which would be their home, and you would be their parents.

What a crazy, goddam, impractical idea! Where would you ever get the money to do a thing like that, and how would you ever earn a living! Where do you get such ideas! Don't you understand anything about the realities of life? After all we've done to teach you the proper values? Where did you get such an idea? Certainly not from us, not from your parents! Good God! You might as well go all through college and medical school and do an internship and residency and then decide to become a medical missionary in...Bangladesh. Did you hear anyone say...Bangladesh?

What we're saying, of course, is that the "crazy" ideas you kids have didn't come from nowhere. Certainly you're going to be influenced by the current scene, by what ideas are prevalent in your social environment, **but there is very often expressed in your own plans or dreams the very plans or dreams your parents had when they were your age.** If your parents had gone on to develop and actually carry out these plans, there's a good chance that you'd be on to something else, moving ahead to new ideas, which is the way with life. But if your parents had to give them up, as is so commonly the case, they didn't forget them, but shoved them into the limbo of their memory, where they are neither remembered nor forgotten.

Somehow or other, by innuendo or by indirection, by denial or by prohibition, your parents managed to get across to you what was just outside the grasp of their own awareness, and gave you instructions to carry out those projects that they themselves had never completed. No, they were not aware that they were doing this. So when you come up with those "outlandish" ideas, they are likely to express their customary horror, failing completely to realize what good kids you are, and how you really listen to your parents. But from their point of view, you are hearing too much, things they never intended you to hear, messages they didn't realize they were sending.

You've probably heard the expression, "The apple never falls far from the tree." Well, we're describing how that peculiar plant magnetism works. Indeed, when your parents note what kind of apple you're turning into, isn't it just like them to deny that they're the apple trees!

14

The Adult Moratorium
(Continued)

When your parents got married there were a whole lot of things they hadn't worked out. Your dad was doubtless earning a fairly reasonable living in some reputable line of work, but that did not mean to him that he was going to spend his whole life doing that particular job. Your mother was probably also employed, but there's a fair chance that she hadn't completed all the education she would have liked, and looked forward to a later opportunity to complete some degree and get into a more satisfying position.

It wasn't only in the education-work area that your parents hadn't resolved things. There's a good chance that they hadn't done all the roaming they'd longed for. And maybe they hadn't made love to everyone they'd wanted to, or in every way they'd wanted to. But they made up their minds to marry each other and decided that they wouldn't worry about everything they hadn't done.

We would like to refer back to that last sentence: "But they made up their minds to marry each other and decided that they wouldn't worry about everything they hadn't done." It's not a great sentence, but it was easy to write. That is, it's part of the great tradition of "That's easy for *you* to say." But how do you actually *do* it? It's like the coach saying, "I know you flunked your History exam yesterday, totalled your car last night, and your girl left you, but I want you to *forget* all that and go out there and play a good game!"

How do you forget things that are important to you? How do you forget the bikes and the cars and the guys and the girls and the clothes and the jobs you wanted and didn't get? How do you forget the times you wanted someone to notice you and be nice to you or recognize you or realize you felt bad about something? How do you make yourself decide that something isn't really important to you when you know all along it is?

What happens to all our wants, our hopes, our lusts, our dreams? Do they just go away because someone says we can't have them, or that we only get a choice of one from Column A, or that you have to give up something to get something? Do we just stop wanting?

These are questions to which we all know the answer. No, we don't stop wanting. No, the wanting doesn't go away. But of course we don't spend our entire conscious life thinking of everything we didn't get (maybe some of us do!), because we're busy concentrating on other things (maybe that's why some of us can't concentrate!). We actually do keep ourselves busy doing all kinds of things which result from some decision we made, or which was made for us.

But it is true that we don't usually spend all our time worrying about what we didn't get. And it is easier not to think about these things if we have something to keep us occupied. Even so, *the wanting doesn't go away.* Where does it go? It goes underground. Just below the level of consciousness, so that it can always pop up again. It goes into what some people call the Subconscious Mind, or the

Preconscious, or the Unconscious—or into our dreams at night: it goes somewhere inside us where it isn't always so obvious, so we don't always have to think about it, but it doesn't go away.

One of the things about being an adult, especially when you're married and have children, is that there's always plenty to do to keep you busy. There's not quite so much time to think about everything you didn't get. As a busy person, you don't sit around and mope and moan. This, of course, is the American Way, sometimes indistinguishable from the Work Ethic or the Puritan Ethic: *don't sit around feeling sorry for yourself; get off your butt and do something to make your life better.*

So here we have all these adults, fresh from their adolescence, scurrying about trying to keep their life and their family's life together, trying to establish a home, trying to make ends meet, trying to get ahead, even trying to have fun. But essentially, everyone is very, very busy, and no one has any time to think about "philosophy" or "values" or "self-actualization" (becoming what you really "could" become, if you could). In a manner of speaking, they're too busy with important things to have any time for "important" things.

Suddenly we find ourselves in a semantic mess: a problem deriving from the meaning of word-symbols. When we say "important," we also have to say: important for *what*, or important for *whom*, or important *by whose standards*. Otherwise all we can do is argue endlessly with each other. Certainly no one will deny that questions about the Purpose of Life, and about what is really Good are important. But no one can deny that earning a living or taking out the garbage is important: just try not having any money for a while, or try letting the garbage accumulate for a couple of weeks, and the "importance" of these matters becomes self-evident. Certainly both kinds of issues are important, but at different times and in different contexts.

A famous psychoanalyst, Erik Erikson, said that the adolescent is granted a kind of *moratorium:* society customarily permits him a period of delay in facing up to the problems of life (like supporting a family), giving him an opportunity to be romantic, to dream dreams, to hang around the pizza parlor, and to take his car apart. He is allowed to observe the universe, to question, and to withhold final judgment. This is viewed by so-called practical people as a kind of luxury that people with everyday responsibilities can ill afford. Hence the adolescent may be considered idealistic rather than realistic.

But it's most interesting that during the relatively brief history of ideas (only a few thousand years compared with possibly hundreds of millions of years that man has been on earth), the terms "ideal" and "real" have flip-flopped back and forth a number of times. For thinkers like Plato and Schopenhauer, *ideas* are the *real* things, and especially for Plato, *things* are just more or less incidental *examples* or *representations* of ideas. For pragmatists like William James and John Dewey, however, nothing is consequential unless it *works,* that is, unless it's *practical.* So from the Platonic point of view, the ideas or ideals of adolescents are the real thing, and what goes on in the marketplace is kind of trivial (which, in case you're interested, is derived from the Latin word *trivia,* for three roads, or the intersection of three roads, or a fork in the road, where people would come together and gossip about unimportant things, like at an Elks convention—unless you happen to be an Elk, in which case the "trivia" is important *to you*).

Now, you can twist the whole thing around and say that adolescents are concerned with ideas, ideals and *values*, which are the really important things in life. Of course no one has been able to answer all the questions that kids can raise, and therefore the adolescent goes right on into adult life without having settled anything important.

Mainly he hasn't settled his own questions about what his own life is about, or what he really stands for or hopes to accomplish. So, in a sense you might say that as an adolescent he is really struggling with burning questions about the meaning of existence. But when he takes on adult responsibility (job, home, family) he no longer has to think about the big questions; he merely has to buckle down and work at putting out the many small fires of industrialized society. If you follow this line of reasoning, you come to the possibly surprising conclusion that it's really the adult himself who's given the moratorium, that it's the adult who can bury himself in work, career, and family-raising, and never have to give a thought to what he really "should" be doing, to what he had set out to do, to what really mattered to him.

By now we understand that **nothing is forgotten, nothing is buried. No one sells out, no one goes over to the other side. Adults are people who do what they have to do; and there's no point in saying that they cop out, that they're lacking in courage, or that they have no sense of values.** The scene shifts, figure becomes ground, the focus is on the stage set rather than on the actors. But the life cycle continues to turn; what *was* no longer is, but perhaps it will be again, though in a slightly different form. And doubtless its appearance will be unexpected, perhaps at first unrecognized. But it will be there, as it has been there all along. So don't leave now; stick around a while longer.

15

The Second Identity Crisis: III. The Reverberating Triangle

Some painful events occur swiftly, as with a shot or a blow or a slash. But intimate interpersonal events, producing even greater psychic anguish, may develop so gradually or imperceptibly that no one can tell when they actually happened. We do not know, to be specific, precisely when the adult moratorium begins, nor do we know very exactly when it ends. We do know, vaguely, that it begins with a dawning realization that someone (me?) is going to have to get a job, that Sally is no longer willing to live with John without a commitment, that John realizes that Sally wants to have a baby and that he has to make up his mind if he can live with this. Decisions must be made; impractical hopes, idle speculation, wishful thinking must be put aside, and with them potentially useful ideas, valued and valuable aspirations, and long-range plans for which the first step may not now be taken.

So the adult moratorium begins with a housecleaning and an attic-stuffing (because we're generally unable to throw away mental accumulations once and for all, except possibly by the use of electric shock). And the adult moratorium ends with all the stuck-away goodies being brought down somehow from the attic. Sometimes this may come about quite literally. Someone (you?) may be rummaging around in the attic and come upon Mom's or Dad's old diaries or notebooks and bring them down into the current living part of the house. Who knows in advance how these once-secreted mysteries will be received? Will your parents laugh or be angry, or be startled? Will they see these words written so long ago as part of themselves or as utterly alien documents?

But more commonly the past is brought to the present by you yourself, or by your brother or by your sister. Let's say your sister Ann is 17 and that she's been seeing one guy pretty regularly. Last Saturday night they had a date and stayed out all night. By Sunday morning your mother was cold, stiff, trembling, and by her own account, almost dead from fear, horror and shame. Your father hadn't been too upset at first, but as your mother got increasingly panicky, he began to get defensive and protective of your mother. So when Ann finally did come home and your mother began to chill her marrow, your father further castigated her with threats of excommunication from the family.

Ann defended herself gamely, but she was no match for her parents. However, she did manage fairly coolly to explain to Mother and Father that staying out all night resulted from a bizarre and highly improbable series of events, that there indeed was a time when she could have let them know, but she let the moment slip away and didn't have another chance, and then they were all out on a boat with no telephone, and she was sorry they worried but she was here safe and sound, so what was there to be upset about?

Mother said, icily, "You know perfectly well what there is to worry about." Father nodded.

Ann said, or rather blurted, "Mother, it's about time you knew I've been having sex with boys since I was fourteen." She ran to her room. Her mother shrieked. Her father went pale.

Mom couldn't stop shrieking, so Dad had to take her to the family doctor, who gave her a tranquilizer by injection and told her that teenage sex was quite a common phenomenon nowadays. When the tranquilizer wore off Mom began shrieking again, so the family doctor recommended that she see a psychiatrist. The psychiatrist talked with your mother, and also with your father, quite a few times and reached several tentative conclusions.

The psychiatrist's first conclusion was that your mother was overreacting to Ann's sexual activities. This did not mean that the psychiatrist was personally in favor of 14-year-old girls engaging in sexual relations; it meant that he knew that this is something that is happening in many cases, and that somehow or other the adult generation, the parents of these kids, have to learn to live with the realities of existence. Nothing is accomplished by adults going around shrieking their heads off!

His next question had to do with *why* your mother was so upset. He learned that she herself had been very interested in sex when she was 14, masturbated, and did what they used to call "heavy petting" (EBI: everything but intercourse). But her parents, your maternal grandparents, were very strict, and really put the fear of God into her, so that she could never, never, perform the sex act outside of marriage no matter how badly she wanted to. This resulted in your mother suffering from a variety of aches and pains, cramps and pelvic congestion, difficulties with sleeping and eating, and of course, with her menstrual periods, which were disastrous. Furthermore, when she did marry

your father, their sexual adjustment was extremely difficult, and your father was so dissatisfied that he began to
look elsewhere. As a matter of fact, after a few drinks he'd
find your sister Ann sexually desirable, but this had never
become an actual problem in the family. (But it could.)

Now, all of this about Mom (and Dad) may or may not
explain why Ann has been sexually open. But that isn't
what we've been trying to account for just now; our focus
has been on how and why adults react to the behavior of
their adolescent children. We're saying that it's the adolescent in the adult, the part that's been stored in the attic, that responds so dramatically to the new situation.
We see this as a triangle of forces. At one point in the
triangle is the adult parent, going about his business, pro-
tected by the adult moratorium from having to think
about all the unresolved problems of his adolescence.
The totality of these unresolved problems make up "the-
adolescent-in-the-adult," which is at the second point in
the triangle. Ordinarily the connection between the adult
and the adolescent-in-the-adult isn't in use; the potential
is there, but most of the time it isn't activated. At the third
point in the triangle, of course, is the adolescent himself
(or herself), you, or your brother or sister. The connection
between you and your parent, obviously, is always in use
(is it ever!).

What is weird about this particular triangle is that there
are real people at only two of the points: you and your
parent. At the third point is *someone who once was* but
who no longer has a valid place in the world, having been
displaced somewhat arbitrarily by your parent's *leap* into
adulthood. We emphasize the "leap" aspect because it
implies that your parent wasn't quite ready for the move;
it is as though, scared half to death, he held his nose and
took the plunge.

Another thing that makes it weird is that one of the participants in the triangle is a ghost. It is our understanding of ghosts that they continue to wander the earth because the person they once were came to an untimely end: he or she died with very important unfinished business. Well, if your parents had finished their adolescent business before leaping into adulthood, there wouldn't be these ghosts hanging around!

Anyway, what gets the triangle activated is your getting into a situation that reverberates with one of the problems that the ghost hasn't resolved. This gets the whole triangle humming and shaking as though it's about to take off on a space flight. Your parent finds out about what you're into, and he looks as though he's seen a ghost! No wonder Ann's mother couldn't stop shrieking!

Unfortunately, or fortunately (as the case may be), we don't have an available list of all the things you might do that are capable of spooking one or both of your parents. One reason for this (not having a list) is that almost anything might set the thing off; another reason is that you can't live your whole life in fear lest your parents throw a fit over something you've done.

We assume that you'll live your life with reasonable good sense, and that nevertheless you'll get screamed at by one or both parents. Part of the time this will be because you goofed, because you knowingly or unknowingly got out of bounds. But not always. *A good part of the time you will be yelled at because of your parent's problems: because of something they did or didn't do once upon a time, and not because of something you did or didn't do yesterday.*

If one of your parents shrieks when they find out about something you've done, check it out with some other people you trust. If what you've done sounds reasonable to them, it's quite likely that your parent has seen a ghost from the past.

Now, we know that you likely have two parents, and each won't always react the same as the other (and vice versa). And of course you realize that it's considered good parental practice for them to cover up any differences they have, and to discuss them in private, with the result that these differences may never be expressed to you. Naturally both parents may not be haunted by the same ghosts.

For example, when Ann's mother was shrieking, her father was getting in his digs, but he was quieter about it. This was because Ann's mother was shrieking. If she'd been calmer, they might have heard him shouting. Why would he have been so steamed? You might as well ask why he finds his daughter sexually attractive, because the two questions are most intimately related, are they not? And is the explanation not to be found among his own ghosts? And isn't this why parents don't tell kids the truth about sex?

There's another way to look at this that may be a little more comforting than the feeling that we are all either haunted or about to be haunted. It's not really much more comforting, but it tends to put parents in a more sympathetic light. And since most of you are going to be parents someday, it may be comforting to know that it's conceivable that *your* kids may be able to view you sympathetically.

How does a little kid feel as he's leaving an amusement park, where he's been through the Fun House and ridden the Rocket, the Satellite, the Trip to the Moon, Sockem,

Dodgem, and the Whip, and he sees another little kid just going in? Does he feel superior for having been there already? Or does he feel envious of all the thrills and chills the other kid is about to experience? Quite possibly a little of both. And how does a parent feel when his children have become full grown and are manifesting their full beauty and strength and vigor? Pretty proud? And how does he feel if he's getting a little paunchy and if he puffs when he walks up a flight of stairs and has to use the golf cart? And how does he feel if he's already had the biggest chances of his life but didn't recognize them until they'd passed—except for one, which he saw, responded to, and muffed? Pretty sick, right? So maybe there's a good chance that he's envious of his kids.

But there's an even better chance that he's kind of sad about life generally, that he has developed a fuller picture of how we are born, grow up, have children, raise them, and then ourselves run down. And he doesn't only see himself as part of this, he also sees you, his own kid, as part of this.

Indeed there may be some relationship between the depth of the adult moratorium and the likelihood of either seeing a ghost or becoming depressed when your kids grow up. It may be that the more the adult has to cut himself off from his own adolescent yearnings, the more likely he is to have them come back to haunt him. The solution to this seems fairly obvious. *Never lose touch with where you are today.* Indeed, wouldn't it be most desirable for each of us to maintain continuous contact with all parts of his historical self? For aren't we always everything we always were? Probably you've read J. D. Salinger's *Catcher in the Rye.* In it, the young hero, Holden

Caulfield, speaks of "phonies." And what is a "phony" other than someone out of touch with himself—with his *real* self? Of course plenty of phonies seem to get away with it, but a phony mostly fools himself, which is too bad for him because that's the only person he really cares about.

16

How To Survive For The Rest Of Your Life (At Least Through Tomorrow)

The encouraging thing about all this is that here you are, going through it for the first time, and if you play the right tapes you can derive much of the benefit of having been here before. Because inside you is the adult that you are going to be, and if you can learn to look inside you, and if you can listen to your parents and learn where they're coming from, then you can start to fit the pieces into that big puzzle out there.

Because in not too much time you're going to have to make some kind of decision. And how you handle that decision is going to determine whether or not you'll have it together thirty or forty years from now or if, as you slog through the muck and mire, you leave three sets of tracks, the middle one being made by your chin. Or at least that's how it feels when you get clobbered by a middle-age depression. That may seem like a long way off, but believe us, it crawls up on you!

Since we don't want anything like that to happen, let's take a look at some practical principles. There are only four, which eventually can be reduced to one, because the first three cancel each other out. Here they are.

148

1. Don't plan your life or make your decisions so that you will either be *like* your parents or like the *opposite* of your parents. In *both* cases your outcome will be determined merely by how your parents think or do things.

2. Your decisions have to be based on what you're good at doing and what can give *you* satisfaction.

3. Remember that in a frightening number of cases, what you think is good for *you* will turn out to be unconsciously determined by what your parents want or don't want.

4. Really make an attempt to understand your parents as fallible, flawed, but 3-dimensional people. Attempt to get behind the parental masks they wear. Try not to be too intimidated by the real or imagined power they have. And try to put off your adolescent mask of belligerence or blaséness or whatever kind of mask you wear to let them know that they can't hurt you anymore and that you really don't care.

What we are prescribing is very difficult and takes some time to achieve. But it can be done and there's a lot in it for you, namely, your independence, your being able to march to your own tune—your not being fettered by things from your past and your parents' past that you don't understand.

Certainly we know it's difficult. We want you to take off your masks and to help your parents take off theirs, for all of you to make yourselves vulnerable. *First you've got to get in touch with your own feelings, because if you don't know how you really feel about things, how can you make the right moves, ask the right questions?*

It would be nice if we could concentrate on pleasant feelings, like love and satisfaction, but before we can get to the good things, all of us have to deal with the usually more unpleasant feelings of anger and fear.

Sometimes it's hard to tell whether we're angry, or afraid, or what. And sometimes the feelings can't be separated, especially when the feelings have to do with parents. Because if you get angry at your parents there may be undesirable consequences, which might be something to be afraid of. That doesn't mean that you're consciously afraid of what your parents might do to you; it might mean fear of losing their support, and then you'd have to face the world alone even though you might not be ready for it. It doesn't mean that there necessarily will be undesirable consequences, or that you should be afraid of your parents, but if you feel that way it's bad enough.

The reason why it's so important to know what your feelings are—and why—is that no one can think clearly when he is angry or afraid, and in order to make decisions you have to think clearly.

Now, when you're vulnerable, you're exposed and without defenses and thus easy prey for someone who may want to hurt you. It's very scary for anyone to feel vulnerable, more so even when we feel more vulnerable than those around us. So you have to do it slowly. No hidden tricks. No cards up the sleeves. Very carefully. And you're probably going to have to take the major risk at first. That is, you're going to have to take the lead. To do this you'll have to have your act together—handling your responsibilities as well as you can. And you will need to approach your parents with genuine curiosity, compassion and sympathy. If they sense you want to "get" something on them, they'll clam up. If they think you want to ridicule them or mock them, they won't cooperate. So you must approach them in a straight and sincere manner, to let them know that you want to hear them out, that you are old enough and interested enough to want to know what they're really up against, to learn about their failures, frustrations, quandaries, hopes, regrets, fears.

Sometimes you may need outside help. You may find it difficult if not impossible to say the things you think you have to say to your parents. It could be your problem in misjudging your parents' defensiveness and capacity to hear what you have to say. Or it could be your parents' problem in their being overly defensive or sensitive and overly "parental": not wanting to hear your point of view. Or more commonly, it could be a combination of your and your parents' problem. As we have talked about earlier, there can be a real tangle of mutual miscommunication and misunderstanding that spirals and knots into something truly horrible. You find yourself damned if you say something, anything, and damned if you keep your mouth shut and say nothing. If you're in this situation you probably feel sullen and angry and probably are counting the hours and days before you can leave home. But it might be a long wait—several months or even years—and it certainly isn't the best way to leave home under any circumstances.

In such instances when you feel you can't make contact with your parents, get hold of someone else who may be able to give you some support and understanding and may be able to show you the way. Brothers and sisters, especially if they're older and have been through the mill, may be helpful. Relatives like aunts and uncles and cousins can be worth talking to, as can school or religious counselors and (some) neighbors. Mostly, though, you're likely to be able to talk to respected friends your own age, of your own peer group.

We have to say people "may" be helpful, rather than "will" be, because there's no certainty that anyone will be able to fill the bill. And, above all, you have to use discretion with whomever you talk. You don't want to seek out someone who will blab or use what you say as material for gossip or ridicule. And you don't want someone who will automatically agree with everything you say to make you feel good or so that you will bolster them up in parallel circumstances. And you definitely want to avoid those "pied pipers"—those cruel misleading people who might want to turn you against your parents for their own ends. There may be people, sometimes older and seemingly mature—who seem to have all the answers about parenting and who might want you to see your parents in the worst possible light—maybe for their own ends.

Your next question, logically, is "How can I know who is reliable and trustworthy and who is not?" Well, it's not as difficult as all that, assuming that you're not so hot-headed or hurt that you lose all perspective, all judgment. *Seek out those who have a good track record and seem to be fairly reasonable. Seek someone whom you respect (and perhaps whom your parents might respect)* rather than someone who is flashy or, like a weathervane, changes direction each time the wind changes. And seek someone who will hear you out and not be too quick to offer his opinion and recommendation.

You may also find a hidden benefit in sharing your concerns in this manner: that is, in having to put your ideas and feelings into words and in attempting to communicate them to someone else, *you may learn things about yourself and your parents* and thus modify some of your ideas.

The ultimate and ideal goal of all this seeking help is to be able *to get back to your parents, to understand them better and to get them to understand themselves and you better.* When this happens, we feel you'll be in a better position to grapple with the big decisions you've got to make for yourself. The big decisions that we're talking about are things like quitting school and getting a job or taking a year off to travel, or going to college or not, or deciding what kind of job or profession you're going into, or deciding to have a baby. These are big things because they determine what the rest of your life is going to be like.

When you're about to make a decision it's easy to think of all the good things that could happen, of all the good feelings you're going to have. And that's OK, because if we only thought of all the things that could go wrong, no one would ever do anything! The important thing is *not to decide things when you're uptight.*

The big question is, how do you know when you're uptight? This is important, because people often don't realize when they are uptight.

There are a couple of reasons for this. The first reason is that it isn't cool to be uptight, and since it's important to be cool, people like to think that they're cool, and they get so worried about being cool that they don't notice how uptight they are. That applies to everybody.

But there's an even more powerful reason than that, and it derives from the kind of culture we live in. In Western civilization and perhaps even especially in the U.S., it isn't the style for people to be in touch with their feelings. We live in an outward-directed, or thing-directed, or action-oriented society, and there doesn't seem to be much payoff to looking inside yourself and trying to understand your feelings.

Aha! you say, isn't that why we have imported Meditation and Yoga from the Orient? And aha! we say right back to you, isn't that a wondrous thing! But, we ask further, how do people use Meditation and Yoga? We wonder if a lot of people don't use them as a *cop-out*, to get themselves into a state of being where they block out how they really feel about things, so that they can keep themselves from knowing (a) that they're uptight, and (b) what they're uptight about! When you're in alpha, you're not thinking about anything, and you're on an entirely different mind-track from the business of making decisions.

Meditation is good for reducing a large variety of tensions and may even be helpful in reducing the symptoms of some illnesses, but it can also be used to take your mind off things that maybe you *should* be thinking about. When we say "should" we don't mean that it's your duty or your obligation, or that you have to do it to please us (whom you've never met) or your parents (or their parents), but that there are things out there ahead of you that aren't going away and which may get in your path and cause you to trip over them.

Now the fact that there is a real world out there is nothing to be scared of in itself, but in the course of your growing up you may have developed a fear of coping with things. If you have, it's tough luck, but nothing to be ashamed of, because you probably learned this attitude at home.

Again we have to say that this isn't anyone's fault. We're not blaming your parents and you shouldn't be blaming yourself. But very often people grow up without ever having to face things directly, and very often this is because parents, without realizing it, may set things up so that their kids never really have to face anything. By now you know how come. You know this is because parents are trying to make things easy, retroactively, for the kid in them, and they end up making things too easy for you. That is, they set it up so that you don't have to cope, and you don't get the important experience that you need for later life.

There is another reason why you may have the bad luck to slide through your adolescence without learning to cope. This is because the teenage establishment—you and your buddies—the junior Mafia—have things set up among yourselves so that it can look like you're really working on some big project, when in fact you're goofing off, smoking pot under a banyan tree.

Of course there's nothing that can drive your parents bananas more effectively than the thought that you, their pride and joy, might not make a huge personal success in the outside world. And we now know why: if you succeed, the child in them succeeds; if you fail, the child in them fails.

And that is why your parents' concern about you is often so irrational, and why they so often lead you on twisted paths to nowhere.

And it is also why *you have to handle your own decisions in a truly grownup way.* Because if you go down the tube your parents may go down with you, but you'll be leading the way. On the other hand, if you work it so that things turn out right for you, are you going to begrudge your parents the little bit or lot of happiness they'll get out of it?

After all, it's *you* who will benefit the most if you do things right. And that is the kind of selfishness no one should begrudge you—least of all yourself—because there's something good in it for everyone.